Happily Insured

THE ONLY BOOK
YOU'LL EVER NEED!

Happily Insured

Your Guide to Understanding Insurance and Leading a Stress-Free Life

KAPIL MEHTA

HARPER
BUSINESS

An Imprint of HarperCollins Publishers

First published in India by Harper Business
An imprint of HarperCollins *Publishers* 2022
4th Floor, Tower A, Building No. 10, Phase II, DLF Cyber City,
Gurugram, Haryana – 122002
www.harpercollins.co.in

2 4 6 8 10 9 7 5 3 1

Copyright © SecureNow TechServices Pvt. Ltd 2022.

P-ISBN: 978-93-5629-236-9
E-ISBN: 978-93-5629-241-3

The views and opinions expressed in this book are the author's own and
the facts are as reported by him, and the publishers are not in any
way liable for the same.

Kapil Mehta asserts the moral right
to be identified as the author of this work.

All rights reserved. No part of this publication may be reproduced,
stored in a retrieval system, or transmitted, in any form or by any
means, electronic, mechanical, photocopying, recording or otherwise,
without the prior permission of the publishers.

Typeset in 11/15 Stempel Garamond LT Std
Manipal Technologies Limited, Manipal

Printed and bound at
Thomson Press (India) Ltd

Dedicated to
the giants in insurance, from whom I learnt what matters most.
Perseverance from Charan Singh
Independence from Tony Singh
Empathy from Bob Fallon.

Contents

Introduction

HAVE YOU THOUGHT about when you feel the happiest? And stress-free? It's when you face a challenge head-on and overcome it. The challenges may be major in areas concerning career, education, health or finances; or minor. Your happiness comes from realizing that obstacles and difficulties are surmountable. Consistently overcoming difficulties builds confidence. The challenges of everyday life don't go away but your self-belief goes up. This then is the secret to being worry-free and reducing your stress.

But how does one systematically overcome challenges? There are things within your control, but it is those problems that are outside your control that create the maximum tension. If you can't control what the world throws at you, how can you bring order into your life? This is where insurance steps in. Insurance can completely take away many of the uncontrollable obstacles you will face in your life. It brings order to an intrinsically chaotic world.

Welcome to the world of insurance. No matter what you do or where you live, chances are that you have bought an insurance product at some point in your life. So, does this topic need a full-fledged book? Isn't insurance something that you already know about and can easily buy? It is heavily advertized and ubiquitous advisers can guide you whenever you want. Surely you can just pick a good insurance? Unfortunately, that is not the case at all.

People consistently make major mistakes in planning for and buying insurance; this, even when the underlying principles to buy a good insurance product are simple, logical and have remained unchanged for hundreds of years. So, unfortunately, instead of being an instrument of stress reduction, insurance purchase creates its own additional stress. Over the two decades that I have worked in the field, I have found so much ignorance and stress related to insurance that I had to address the issue. That's why I have written this book. It is a definitive compendium on all that you need to know about insurance.

Read it to understand the principles behind insurance, the practical tools to buying the right products, what to do when you need to make a claim, the laws that safeguard you when you have a problem, and how to get your grievances sorted out. When you finish this book, you'll not only be wiser and aware of the risks you face, but also sure about how to use insurance to eliminate many of those risks. You will save yourself considerable money when buying insurance and also mitigate potential financial losses that you might have. This then will set you firmly on the path of being free of stress.

We think about insurance when there is a problem such as a personal illness, destruction of an asset or a natural calamity close by. The stress of the moment makes us consider if insurance can provide solutions. During the COVID-19 pandemic, demand for health insurance shot up, with the greatest demand coming from people who were already ill. Home insurance enquiries increased materially after the Chennai floods. In difficulties, we assume that insurance will bail us out, but mostly it is already too late to buy insurance and the damage is done. You have to think of risks when they are least, plan for difficulties in good times, hope for the best, but prepare for the worst. Such preparation will allow you to face difficulties head-on.

Insurance eliminates many risks that you might face—ill health, death, accidents, burglaries, vehicle and home damage. When people think of investments they focus on the upsides and on higher than normal returns. I suggest when you think of insurance, focus on the downsides and on higher than normal risk. Preparing for these downsides will leave you more in control, and a sense of security and happiness will soon follow.

Insurance has limitations. Not all problems can be insured against. When a family member dies, insurance can remove the financial uncertainty that often follows, but it cannot substitute for the loss of an integral family member. Life insurance is mostly bought with the purpose of earning a return, as most people find it hard to think of death. In some countries, insurance companies (henceforth, insurers) address this by requesting the person whose life is insured to write a letter that will be delivered to their nominees when they die. The letter becomes not only a valuable memory for those left behind, but also a reminder as to why that person bought insurance in the first place.

Business write-ups highlight the macroeconomic impact of insurance but it is the individual stories that showcase the value of insurance best. This is why I have written about my acquaintances, friends and family. Within these pages you will meet Kalu, a caddie at the Delhi Golf Club and know Vani, a batchmate from IIM Ahmedabad. You will travel back in time to understand my grandmother, who was born in undivided India. You will know what I felt for a retired old man in South Delhi and you will find a kindred soul in an insurance agent.

But the person I would like you to meet most is 'The Lady with Parkinson's (chapter 15). I met her on the streetside, one sunny winter's day in Delhi, as Abhishek, my co-founder at Securenow, and I were walking from our Defence Colony office to Sagar Ratna for lunch. Many years later, I have still not been able to get the lady out of my mind. Where is she now? Was her journey successful?

My purpose in writing this book is to ensure that you think about insurance, plan for it and buy what is best for you. A thoughtful purchase today, will reduce much of your future stress and will allow you to live a happier and more secure life.

Understanding purpose is difficult. For most of my career, purpose has been defined by my place of work—each a fabulous organization and I remain indebted to them. At Unilever, my first job, I sold tonnes of soap in the wholesale markets of Hyderabad. I wanted nothing more than to meet my monthly sales targets. At McKinsey, I was transformed into a crusader for our clients' successes. At Max New York Life and at Prudential, both insurance companies, I pursued the corporate objectives of sales and profits. It is only during the past decade, in my forties, through the people you will meet in this book, that I realized that selling insurance was a noble purpose in itself. And an indispensable tool to living a stress-free life.

The lights in my mind began to switch on after I started writing for *Mint* in 2011. I had left my job as the managing director of Prudential Financial's life insurance company in India and was building SecureNow, an entrepreneurial venture with Abhishek. *Mint* asked me to answer insurance queries from readers and then graduated me to a column on insurance. What I learnt most while responding to readers' queries and writing the column, was the possibility of diverse perspectives.

Insurers, distributors, regulators and policyholders view things differently. Abe Lincoln famously said, 'Be sure you put your feet in the right place, then stand firm.' I have consciously taken the policyholder's view in this book, with the exception of chapters 32 ('The Need for Respect and Reasonable Expectations') and 33 ('The Unsung Heroes Selling Insurance') where I nudge policyholders to treat insurance salespersons better.

Reading about insurance is usually soporific. I credit my son Aditya and my wife Anjali for critically reading, without succumbing to sleep, every bit of insurance writing I have ever done. They have also prevented me from excessive moralizing; they and Cheryl Strayed who wrote *Tiny Beautiful Things*, compiled from a hugely popular column in the United States (US) called 'Dear Sugar'.[i] I love her direct, tongue-in-cheek humour that emerges from her own individual experiences and makes weighty matters seem lighter.

Several of my firsthand experiences also find their way into these chapters. When my daughter was about to leave home for college, I wrote, 'Who Should Be Insured When Your Child Studies Overseas, and How?' (chapter 28). My wife is a doctor and her battles with insurers and large hospitals became the basis for chapters 12 ('How Much Difference Can Selecting a Hospital Make?') and 39 ('The Benefits of Due Process'). I remembered my grandmother in 'How Insurance Gives Dignity' (chapter 54). A family excursion resulted in 'Unfollow Social Media

---

i   Strayed, C. (2012). *Tiny Beautiful Things: Advice on Love and Life from Someone Who's Been There*. New York: Vintage Press.

for Insurance' (chapter 34). My mother's long years of work in mental health found a place in 'Why Insurance Fails People With Mental Illness' (chapter 9).

The book has four sections: Products, Processes, Insurance Documents, and Purpose. Each section has several small chapters that are stand-alone and need not be read in sequence. There are detailed endnotes, most relevant for those interested in the regulations behind insurance or in gossipy backstories.

The facts that you read in here are useful, but more important are the principles behind buying insurance. Those principles are unlikely to change anytime soon.

There have been special moments in my insurance journey. One such was over a decade ago. I was embarking on an insurance-broking business and the rules required two people to clear a regulatory examination. I roped in my father, then seventy-four years old, to take the exam with me. He pored over the study material, worried that his failure would somehow impair my future. We both cleared the exam. More recently, when I took the renewal version of that very examination, one of the questions was an extract from my own writings, where I was asked to comment on what the author could possibly mean. That, I got right. The wheel had come full circle.

I am thin-skinned and many years ago bristled at social get-togethers when people switched-off on being told that I worked in insurance. A newspaper once called insurers, and by inference executives like me, 'godless agents of capitalism'. The credit for making me less godless must go to the lady with Parkinson's.

As you read this book, pause and think about adversities but then quickly switch to the solutions that insurance provides. Having a proper insurance programme in place will lead you to a happier, stress-free life.

PART 1

Products—Managing Risks

1
Health

AS WE GROW older, health becomes a major worry. Not just our own but also that of our parents and children. We want the best medical care for our family but that is expensive. Health insurance, if bought properly and in time, can address this. Unfortunately, in many cases, this does not happen. Consider these situations that I have seen at close quarters. This could be you.

- A young couple had prematurely born twins. They were kept in a paediatric intensive care unit (PICU) for over a month, a total cost of over ₹20 lakh. Sadly, the couple had not bought a health cover that would automatically cover newborns.
- A friend's seventy-year-old father was hospitalized for asthma. But his insurance claim was rejected, because he had

not disclosed a heart condition several years earlier when buying the insurance. The treatment cost ₹10 lakh.

- A colleague, about forty years old, forgot to renew the family's health insurance. Two months later his wife was diagnosed with breast cancer. The insurer refused to reinstate the insurance and no other insurer would provide cover. Treating the cancer cost ₹4 lakh.

- A young lady in her mid-forties had a robotic cyst removal. This procedure cost about ₹4 lakh, twice the cost of a non-robotic surgery. The claim was not paid because the policy did not cover (i.e., excluded) robotic surgeries.

- A friend who has worked in companies all his life decided to venture into his own business. Previously, he had always been insured by his employer's group health insurance. Now, at fifty-three, he has had to buy a personal health insurance. This has cost him over ₹1 lakh because of the hypertension he recently developed.

- A friend died in the pandemic. However, the insurer settled only a part of the claim citing a Delhi Government restriction on room tariff. The family had to pay ₹20,000 out of their pocket.

- A colleague disclosed his heart condition while porting his insurance, yet his claim was denied. Unfortunately, he had no evidence that the health condition had been declared and had to pay his treatment cost of about ₹1.5 lakh himself.

This section shows you how to buy health insurance, including when you suffer from any illnesses. Also, which insurers to select. You will read about what information to disclose but also what not to. Health insurance has some limitations that you will learn about. It is best to know those limitations now, than be surprised later. The central theme, though, is to buy a regular mediclaim insurance, with the right sum assured, as soon as possible.

What Matters Most in Health Insurance?

How do you decide what matters when buying health insurance? There are over 100 products and if you count add-ons and customizations the options run into thousands. Getting access to product information is difficult. Most of you will not be able to download all the product brochures and calculators. And even if you did, how would you know what to focus on? To make matters worse, the impact of a wrong purchase will be felt several years later, when you make a claim.

Or, imagine getting hospitalized only to be told that half the cost will not be paid because there is a disease-cap, which sets an upper limit, less than the sum assured in the insurance; or that you are only eligible for a shared room; or even finding out that you could have saved thousands of rupees by buying a different insurance product.

The answer to the question, what matters in health insurance, has remained unchanged over the years. Certain product features matter the most, and this is also the collective view of people who understand health insurance intimately. These four features are:

- **The price:** the annual cost of buying a particular health-insurance package.
- **Room-rent capping:** the limit on the amount of room rent the insurance company will pay, in case you are hospitalised.
- **The number of years pre-existing conditions are excluded:** The term 'pre-existing conditions' refers to any diseases or adverse health conditions you had at the time of

purchasing insurance. 'Excluded' means that even though you have informed the insurance company of these health conditions, your insurance will not pay for any treatment or hospitalization because of these conditions, for a fixed period of time after purchase (usually two to four years).

- **The insurance company's track record**: Specifically, if the insurer pays claims in a timely manner (or not).

In March 2020 the Insurance Brokers Association of India (IBAI) surveyed its members on health insurance.[1] This survey was to be part of a health insurance conference organized by the Federation of Indian Chambers of Commerce and Industry (FICCI), subsequently postponed due to Covid-19. The survey included thirty-eight respondents with deep experience in the sector, with 50 to 75 per cent of their business originating from health insurance.

On what matters most, 53 per cent said product features, 24 per cent said price, and 23 per cent said payment of claims. The fact that such a sizeable proportion rooted for product features reinforces that purchasing health insurance is a high engagement decision where you should deeply understand your purchase and pay more for the right features.

The survey probed specific product features that were relevant, using the Net Promoter Score (NPS) approach.[2] The NPS reports the difference between promoters and detractors. A positive score indicates that more people are willing to strongly recommend the product feature, and a negative score implies that there are more detractors than recommenders. The two product features found to have the highest NPS scores were: (i) 82 per cent in favour of a shorter exclusion (no insurance cover) period for adverse health conditions that existed at the time of purchasing the insurance policy, and (ii) 66 per cent in favour of no limits on the room rent claimable for a hospital stay.

Experts recognize that most claims are rejected because they are related to treatment of pre-existing adverse health conditions. The experts also prefer insurance packages that come with the minimal two-year period (of not offering coverage for diseases and health conditions that existed at the time of purchase of the insurance package). Similarly, a low or no room-rent cap is preferred because then the deductions from the hospital bill (items that the insurance will not pay for) are small. The negative impact that room-rent caps currently have, is expected to reduce as the Insurance Regulatory and Development Authority of India (IRDAI) has initiated regulation in this regard.

The lowest rated product features were international cover (minus 34 per cent) and wellness (minus 29 per cent) respectively, both significantly negative. This is unexpected because both these features are prominent in the marketing propositions of insurers. Why are these scores so low then?

International cover is rated poorly because there is insufficient evidence of claims paid and the underlying claim processes can be complicated. Some insurers allow only reimbursement, others only the cashless option. Still others allow treatment only in certain countries, and in some cases only treatments for certain diseases are allowed. It is clear though that there is a niche segment that would like the opportunity to get treated overseas. A few insurances allow such treatment with minimal restrictions and there is likely to be more innovation in this area.

The issue with wellness is that the tangible benefit can be hard to discern. Experts are concerned that wellness may be a marketing pitch more than a true proposition. For example, many insurers offer a free health check-up. However, the tests covered by the check-up are basic and may be restricted to certain labs. The labs charge full rates if you want to add new tests and so the total cost can be prohibitive. Many insurance plans offer discounts on product purchases, but these are widely available to you through various platforms outside the insurance. Some insurers follow a point system of credit but there are limitations on the final benefit. The full value of wellness will come about when the benefits can be used in a frictionless manner and have a significant impact on the sum assured and on premium.

The MoneyControl SecureNow Health Insurance Ratings (MCSHIR),[3] developed by SecureNow for *Moneycontrol*, gives 40 per cent weightage to product features, 35 per cent to claims and 25 per cent to pricing. This is based on insurers' perspectives, market surveys and direct feedback from policyholders.

In buying health insurance we must focus on the things that matter most: product features, followed by claims and price. But once you know what to focus on, how do you decide the sum assured (the maximum amount you can get when you file a claim) and product type?

Your First Two Decisions

A simple algorithm can help you get started in buying your health insurance. Algorithms are systematic rules that can solve most problems. Google's PageRank forms the basis of web search; travelling-salesman algorithms help schedule flights; poor-quality-queueing algorithms explain why I always have the longest wait for elevators in Gurugram.[4]

Here is a simple algorithm to decide the right health product structure. This algorithm is derived from my responses to the hundreds of health insurance queries I get each year: What sum assured to buy? Is a family-floater better or individual insurance? Should I buy a top-up plan?

I used to offer specific, personalized responses to each query but soon saw a pattern repeat itself. Following this pattern of decisions will help you buy the right health insurance.

- **First, decide the target sum assured:** This is easier said than done. An experienced underwriter explained that one gets to know the sum assured is inadequate only when it runs out.[ii] There is, however, an excellent surrogate to set the sum assured and that is the cost of a Coronary Artery Bypass Graft (CABG), commonly known as a heart bypass surgery.

  CABG is a common treatment for cardiac disorders a disease category responsible for the largest number of deaths. The Public Health Foundation estimates that 8 per cent of all hospitalization cases, second only to accidents and other injuries, are due to cardiovascular disease. This is one of the most expensive ailments to treat. Last year, I saw about a hundred CABG insurance claims. These were generally the most expensive claims and cost between ₹2.5–8 lakh.[iii]

  Health cover that you buy today must cater to costs over at least ten years. At current medical inflation of about 15 per cent, a CABG procedure ten years from now will cost ₹10 lakh if you go to a 'no-frills but reputed' hospital and ₹30 lakh in a 'five-star' facility. Ask yourself which hospital you are likely to go to and set your sum assured accordingly. I have used ten years as a benchmark, rather than a longer period, because experience suggests that medical advancements are likely to keep costs in check beyond this.

  You need to decide if your target sum assured should be bought on a family or on an individual basis. Counter-intuitively, in most cases, I find that the individual sum assured is cost-effective. That's because insurers price

---

ii   Underwriting is the process by which an insurer assesses an application, decides whether to issue the insurance, and sets price.

iii   ₹1 lakh = About USD 1300

family-floaters on the age of the oldest person,[iv] whereas other family members may be much younger. Also, the probability of a claim in a family-floater is higher than in individual insurances.

- **Decide product type:** The variety of product structures is confusing. Mediclaim pays for hospitalization, top-up plans pay up after a certain minimum expense is crossed, critical-illness insurances benefit only if you get specific diseases, and personal accident insurance covers medical expenses only in case of injury.

  Buying a regular mediclaim is first priority. This pays for hospitalization costs. If you do not already have one, buy any 'A' rated product in the Health Insurance Ratings (MCSHIR) done by SecureNow.[5] These comprehensive ratings factor-in premiums, exclusions, the claims track record and product restrictions.

  If you do have mediclaim then continue with that. Regulations require that all health insurance products meet a minimum standard of cover and lifelong renewability; the longer you hold insurance the more difficult it is for an insurer to reject claims.

  Your current mediclaim cover is likely to be far less than the target sum assured. Bridge the gap with a top-up plan that pays costs above a certain minimum threshold (also called deductible). Such top-up plans are cheaper than regular mediclaim insurances because the insurer's liability is lower. Buy any top-up plan with a 'Super top-up' structure; set deductibles in the top-up insurance equal to your current insurance and the sum assured to bridge the gap between

---

iv   'Family-floater' is an insurance that covers the entire family under one policy and sum assured. This is different from an individual insurance where the sum assured can only be used by one person.

your target and current insurance. So, if you have a large claim then your current mediclaim cover will pay upto the maximum sum assured in that policy and additional expenses will be paid for by the top-up insurance.

So what is the 'Super top-up' structure? It goes by various trade names 'Super top-up', 'Enhance', 'Super' but is not 'Super-expensive'. In this plan deductibles can be set-off across ailments and are not restricted to one hospitalization.

- **Buy a critical-illness plan:** Critical-illness plans serve several objectives and cover out-of-pocket expenses, non-hospitalization costs and lost income. However, its major benefit is that diseases that do not require hospitalization, also get insured—for example, Alzheimer's, blindness, deafness, stroke, and paralysis. Buy a critical illness plan that covers a large number of diverse diseases, at the very minimum twenty. Make sure the sum assured is equal to the target sum assured on your regular mediclaim.

People who ask me about health insurance tend to focus excessively on price. I am reminded of the 'Greedy Algorithm' taught to us in college. In this, short-term objectives are maximized in the hope that the outcome will be the best. That is a fallacy. Getting health insurance at the lowest price is fine, but it is crucial to get the broad health insurance structure in place first.

Once you have decided on the sum assured and policy type, the next step is to select a specific insurer.

How Unbiased Health Insurance Ratings Help

Changing with the times seems to be the sine qua non for commercial success. Within insurance the refrain, in line with adapting to changed circumstances, is to be more digital, sell byte-size insurance, add wellness and out-patient department

(OPD) benefits, and develop products for specific diseases like dengue, cancer and COVID-19. These are all good things to do, I am sure, but when I look back at the seven years of preparing the medical ratings,[6] the aspects I value most are those that have remained unchanged. These timeless aspects include claim settlement rates, low exclusion period and no restrictions on room type.

Ratings such as the MCSHIR are comprehensive and fact-based. The rating developer has done all the groundwork of data collection and analyses. And, if you agree with the rating criteria, they can quickly help you identify which insurer and also which specific product to select.

Our ratings typically give 40 per cent weightage to product features, 35 per cent to claims and 25 per cent to the premium. Five years ago, our weightage for product features was the same but for claims it was 5 per cent lower and for the premium 5 per cent higher, a minor change. There is a constant debate on the 'correct' weightage for the premium. I think we have found the balance. Product features are the most important, because they decide what you will get when you claim. The claim payment track record is second, because it shows actual delivery on claims, and premiums are third, but not insignificant.

Over the years the ratings of various product features have changed somewhat, but the top two features have always been: (i) the number of years that your insurance policy will not cover any disease(s) you already had at the time of purchasing the insurance, and (ii) the limit your policy sets for your hospital room-rent (any amount over the limit will have to be paid by you).

Wellness features are given a small weight by us, because wellness activities often translate into a specific financial benefit for policyholders that they cannot otherwise get on their own. Such a definition eliminates OPD and pharmacy discounts, because many platforms offer those without insurance. Similarly, providing policyholders with mobile apps or wearables, but with no financial incentive to keep well, does not count. Wellness benefits are counted if they: (i) lead to a reduction in premium; (ii) add points that can be used for purchases. In our annual ratings all health insurance products are evaluated. The only condition for inclusion in the ratings is that the product and its premiums should be available on the insurer's website.

There is no subjectivity in our ratings, they are all fact-based. The information can be verified from public disclosures and the insurer's own website. The math behind our ratings is transparently shared. This insistence on verifiable data also presents issues, the most pressing being that published claims information is at an aggregate level and not segregated by product. Since a large weightage (35 per cent) is given to claims, more refined information would be extremely useful. For example, a good pointer for long-term viability is the Incurred Claims Ratio (ICR), which provides valuable insights into an insurer's business. The ICR is published at an aggregate level by the IRDAI in its annually-updated *Handbook of Insurance Statistics*.

The ICR is the total value of claims paid over total premium collected, and is the main driver of underwriting profit. Devotees of Warren Buffett would have seen the concept described every year in the Berkshire Annual Letters.[v] A low ICR means that claims are not being paid, or that the prices of the insurance policies

---

v   Berkshire Hathaway has published, since 1965, an annual letter for shareholders written by Warren Buffett. These letters are avidly read because they are lucid, honest and often humourous. As insurance is a significant part of Berkshire Hathaway, Mr. Buffett often elegantly explains complex insurance concepts. The letters can be read at https://berkshirehathaway.com/letters/letters.html.

offered are too high. On the other hand, a high ICR suggests that the business is not viable! Government health insurance schemes have claim ratios of 97 per cent which means that the business is mostly making a loss. In terms of performance, there are marked differences between the public and the private sector. For example in health insurance, government insurers had a loss ratio of 103 per cent, whereas stand-alone private health insurers had a loss ratio of 64 per cent.[7]

Overall you should look for the right balance—an insurer should have an ICR that is neither too high nor too low. The cut-off for A-rated products, has consistently been 65 per cent. In 2020, the number of products that met this benchmark reduced. For example, for a forty-five-year-old individual looking for a policy with ₹10 lakh sum assured, the number of products available fell from nine to six in 2020. Similarly, in the category of individual cover of ₹20 lakh for a seventy-five-year-old, the number of products rated A came down from three to two. This is primarily because of two factors: price increases and worsening claims performance.

The best insurances for you to buy are those rated A. Once you have decided on the sum assured and product structure, simply pick any of the A-rated products most accessible to you. Many of these can be bought directly from the insurer's website. If you have a pre-existing health condition then you could widen your search to include B-rated products as well.

As I look back at the past decade, there have been some remarkable improvements in health insurance. Today, contract definitions and exclusions (what all your insurance will not cover) are standardized, the definition of pre-existing health conditions is policyholder-friendly, insurances must be renewable lifelong, premiums cannot be changed for specific persons based on their claims history, and after eight years health insurance-related claims cannot be rejected for any reason other than fraud.

Our ratings provide an easy way to select a specific insurance, because detailed analyses has already been done before scoring products. You should also be reassured by the fact that the law guarantees a high minimum standard in any health insurance product that you may buy. A detailed list of A-rated products can be seen on https://securenow.in/specials/mediclaim-ratings-insurance.

These ratings are for mediclaim insurances that primarily cover actual in-patient hospitalization expenses. However, what should you do to insure for critical illnesses where the out-of-hospital costs can be extremely high and often unrelated to actual medical treatments?

Should You Buy Critical-illness Insurance?

Critical-illness insurances pay a fixed amount if you develop any of the diseases covered. These insurances first made their entry about two decades ago, and were attached to life insurance plans. Most salespersons at the time did not like these insurances because they required several medical tests, which was a major reason for their sales dropping; also, claim settlement was poor. At that time each insurer had their own definition of diseases that were accepted as a critical illnesses, depending upon the reinsurer they worked with. Reinsurers are the companies that insure the insurers illnesses. So, in many insurances, including critical illness plans, when the insurer pays you a claim, they recover that from the reinsurers. Reinsurers play a major role in the way insurance policies are defined and this used to include the definition of critical illnesses. From that tentative start these insurances have come a long way. Health insurers have taken the lead in introducing stand-alone plans that are comprehensive and many insurers have established an excellent track record with regard to the payment of claims.

The incidence of critical illnesses is alarming. I do not need to provide quantitative information. Look at your close family and friends and you'll find instances of cancer and heart disease. It is also evident that these diseases are striking younger people more often. The case to buy critical-illness insurance has never been stronger.

Many of us do not differentiate between a regular mediclaim health insurance and a critical-illness plan. This is a mistake because the two serve quite different objectives and complement each other. Mediclaim reimburses hospital costs, but critical-illness pays a fixed amount independent of cost. Mediclaim covers hospitalization for any reason, but critical-illness pays only for pre-identified diseases. Mediclaim is renewable for life, whereas the critical-illness plan is extinguished after the first claim. The first purchase you make should be the mediclaim, and then supplement that with critical-illness insurance.

The price and the claims-settlement track record are two criteria common for all insurances. However, criteria specific to selecting critical-illness insurances are: the number and type of diseases covered; period for which pre-existing diseases are excluded from the insurance cover; maximum sum assured allowed; and the survival period. The survival period is the number of days that you must live after being diagnosed with a critical illness to be eligible for a claim.

The number of diseases covered range from less than ten and up to forty, in a single insurance. It is not just the number of diseases that is important, but also the kinds of diseases. I prefer critical-illness plans that cover diseases such as blindness, deafness, loss of speech, Alzheimer's,[8] multiple sclerosis, and strokes—because these diseases do not require significant hospitalization. This means you will be able to claim payment, while taking treatment outside the hospital too. In a standard mediclaim insurance, the coverage for these diseases is limited to payment for hospital stays alone.

I am wary of insurances that permanently exclude coverage for the purchaser's pre-existing health conditions, because there is always a niggling worry that a future claim, linked to a pre-existing condition, may be denied. Imagine a situation where many years after buying insurance, a critical-illness claim is turned down because it can be linked to a prior ailment. In regular mediclaim insurances, the regulations do not allow a blanket exclusion for pre-existing ailments for more than four years. Even in critical-illness insurances, some insurers restrict the exclusion period to four years, which is good.

Critical illnesses are expensive to treat. Cancer, organ replacements, CABGs or open-heart surgeries cost over ₹10 lakh. These costs are increasing at over 15–20 per cent each year, which means that a decade from now it may cost over ₹50 lakh to treat a critical illness. That is why a large sum assured helps. Since, all critical-illness plans are renewable lifelong, the insurance you buy today is something you may keep for many years before using.

Critical-illness plans often mandate a survival period of thirty to ninety days, to be eligible for a claim. This refers to the time after being diagnosed that you must survive to be eligible for a claim. So, if you are diagnosed with cancer today, the insurer will wait for the survival period to get over, check if you survived and then pay the claim. I do not like this restriction, because there can be many cases where a person may not survive this period. This is most common in the case of heart diseases and strokes.[9] Some insurers do not require a survival period in their insurance.

Some common exclusions—apart from those I have already described—are: diseases less than the specified severity; early claims in the first ninety days of the insurance; and illness caused by smoking or drugs. The severity of disease has been standardized by the regulator across insurers. Do file a claim within a week or two of being diagnosed with a critical illness. Claim forms are available online.

Most of the information you need to assess a critical-illness product are in the policy's wording, available on the insurer's website. Claims settlement rates are in the public disclosures, but can be more easily accessed through the insurance regulator's annual report.

We once analysed six hundred claims across twenty companies with group health insurance. Fifty of these claims were critical illnesses and fifteen breached the sum assured limit, which meant that patients were paying out of pocket, a situation that a critical-illness plan would have prevented.

I was once discussing the claims pattern of people retired from the armed forces with executives of the Ex-Servicemen Contributory Health Scheme (ECHS), and they said that cancer treatment costs have shown the maximum increase over the years. Should you then be thinking of a separate insurance just for cancer?

What To Do about Sky-Rocketing Cancer Cost?

Given India's large size, we have earned the moniker of being the world capital of most diseases, ranging from diabetes and hypertension to cardiac illness. Which of these causes the most havoc? Two stand out from the dozens of health insurance claims reports that I see each week: infections and cancer.[10]

Mosquitoes and viruses are having a field day because every hospitalization report is filled with infection claims. But these tend to be low-cost, requiring just a day or two of hospitalization. COVID-19 has increased the medical cost of infections but the fact is that most treatments still take place without hospitalization.

Cancer claims though fewer, are exceptionally large in value. We do not need statistics to prove this.

I can count ten instances of cancer amongst close family and friends over the past few years. The highest incidence is of breast cancer. A study by Edelweiss Tokio Life suggests that advanced treatment of cancer costs between ₹10–14 lakh on average. A different study by EY suggests that in 75 per cent of homes in India the treatment cost of cancer is more than the household's annual income. Distress financing or borrowing is highest for cancer. Cancer is also the most frequent reason for the entire sum assured by a health policy, being used up. This is why we must insure for cancer.

Insurers have developed several products to cover cancer costs. The quality of these insurances is uniformly good. There are three broad product types: regular mediclaim, critical-illness, and stand-alone cancer plans.

A regular mediclaim insurance will cover actual cancer-related costs ranging from expensive diagnostics using PET scans, MRIs or other equipment, to treatment including chemotherapy, radiation and post-treatment care. Exclusions vary but items such as hormone treatment, Cyberknife treatment and certain skin cancers are sometimes excluded. These exclusions will reduce as the IRDAI is in the process of setting conditions for what must be covered in health insurance.[11]

The advantage of mediclaim insurance is that it covers all illnesses and not just cancer. However, from the perspective of covering cancer, the issue is that the sum assured is often insufficient because the plans are bought with the intention of covering lower-value hospitalization claims. Also, you must be healthy when you buy mediclaim. As you grow older or develop chronic ailments, insurance becomes more expensive to buy.

Critical-illness insurance was first sold about fifteen years ago, as an add-on to life insurance. However, health insurers have now taken up the concept and introduced several standalone critical illness plans. These plans do not reimburse actual costs but pay a fixed amount if you are diagnosed with cancer, or other listed critical illnesses. These plans also require you to undergo a health test and be relatively fit when buying.

Most recently some insurers have introduced stand-alone cancer plans. Like critical-illness insurances, these pay a fixed amount when you are diagnosed with cancer but have four advantages: (i) they can be issued without a medical test; (ii) the benefit can be paid for an early-stage cancer, compared to critical illness or standard mediclaim plans; (iii) you can have a pre-existing condition unrelated to cancer and still buy the policy; and, (iv) these are economical. Some of these insurances waive future premium requirements if you are diagnosed with early-stage cancer.

Which of these insurances should you buy? Your first preference should be to get the regular mediclaim with a high sum assured, ₹20 lakh or more. This should then be supplemented with a critical-illness cover or a stand-alone cancer plan. The choice will depend upon your health and how much you can pay. At age fifty, a critical-illness plan for an assured sum of ₹20 lakh, will cost about ₹25,000–30,000 per year, whereas a cancer stand-alone insurance will cost between ₹3,000–5,000.

The battle against cancer is daunting. A Ken report[12] states that as per estimates one in three households is likely to be affected by cancer. Also, less than fifteen per cent of cancer cases receive early treatment that could be life-saving. A Novartis-CII report[13] on breast cancer highlights that about half of all breast cancer patients are diagnosed when they are less than fifty years old. Of those that are diagnosed, over 70 per cent are in advanced stages (three and four) where mortality is highest. Insurance can do little to reduce cancer incidence or improve detection. Your priority, then, must be to get yourself screened periodically for cancer.

One of the issues you will face if you fall ill, of cancer or otherwise, is that over half of all healthcare expenses are OPD costs. This includes visits to doctors, diagnostic care and nursing support at home. Shouldn't that also be separately insured?

Is the Hoopla around OPD Insurance Justified?

Mediclaim insurances cover hospitalization and day care procedures. Many personal expenses, however, occur in the OPD and on diagnostic tests. I include the latter in OPD. An MRI can cost ₹10,000, blood tests up to ₹3,000, medication for chronic ailments such as hypertension and diabetes over ₹10,000 a year, and a specialist consultation ₹1,000 per visit. These costs are generally not paid for by insurance.

Insurers hesitate to offer OPD cover for a few reasons. First, it results in a large number of small claims. These are expensive to manage and result in a high workload. Second, pharmacies and diagnostic centres are fragmented, which makes it difficult to build a reliable network. Without such a network, the system is prone to fraud and the technology for pharmacies to interact with insurers is basic. That is why the cashless payment process—so popular during hospitalization—is seldom followed in OPD.

Some OPD costs are covered. Insurers will pay for costs incurred thirty days before and sixty days after hospitalization, within the overall sum assured. Those OPD costs that do not result in hospitalization are not paid. For example, an ultrasound that gives you a clean chit, will not be paid for. An example relevant today is that of a COVID-19 test. If you test positive and are hospitalized, the cost of the diagnostic test is covered, otherwise not. Insurers have now started to introduce separate OPD covers to complement their base plans.

The OPD benefits offered vary by: (i) amount, (ii) nature of expense covered, and (iii) the claims process. Understanding these three aspects will help you decide whether the OPD is worth paying for.

All OPD plans come with a maximum spending limit. These can range from a few hundred rupees to ₹10,000 or more. If a limit is not specified, but the insurer lists the number of consultations or other benefits allowed, you can apply a rough value to that to see what the implicit limits are. The question to ask is if the amount of OPD cover is actually useful. The OPD plans are priced with just a small insurance element. What this means is that if you are getting ₹5,000 as an OPD benefit, then an additional premium of ₹3,000–5,000 will be charged for that.

Some OPD plans allow any medical expense to be claimed. However, more common is some form of restriction. For example, one insurer restricts the benefit to eye and dental care, another to vaccinations. Read the policy wordings regarding OPD carefully to know what is insured.

Finally, insurers will specify a claim process. This specification can make a difference to the usefulness of the benefit. A common restriction is the number of times in a year that a claim can be filed. If you are permitted to file only one or two claims in a year, then you will need to keep your bills carefully throughout the year and claim when allowed. Another type of restriction is when OPD services must be availed only from a list the insurer provides, with approved hospitals or pharmacies. If that is the case then do make sure there are pharmacies located close to you. Generally, it is best to go for those OPD plans that have few process restrictions.

The OPD space is going to develop rapidly over the next few years. Some insurers have introduced products that combine OPD and wellness. Wellness may be in the form of an annual health check-up, or incentives to keep fit. The annual health check-up is now offered by many. Do read the fine print to see what the check-up includes and where it must be conducted.

Often, just the basic tests are paid for and the cost of adding additional tests can be high. There are also a few health cards in the market that offer discounts on OPD services as well as subsidized tele-medicine services.

These new products are a move in the right direction because they shift the focus to prevention. I have two specific suggestions for people with large OPD expenses. The first is to approach a general practitioner (GP) before reaching out to specialists. The time-tested system of first going to the family GP is under strain because many people approach specialists based on their own assessment of issues. This drives their costs up without necessarily resulting in better outcomes. Second, there are likely to be many new OPD-oriented products launched in the market over the next few years, including stand-alone OPD plans. If your health permits, wait to see what these new products are, before you buy.

As mentioned earlier the first health insurance to buy is mediclaim, which should then be supplemented by critical-illness insurance. Once these two plans are in place you should think about your OPD needs.

Purchasing insurance if you are healthy is easy and following a systematic, logical process will result in good buys. But what if you are unwell, perhaps an accident in the past or a chronic disease such as diabetes or mental illness? Will insurers still sell you health insurance?

The Secret to Buying Insurance When You Have a Health Issue.

One would expect that with all the competition in insurance, insurers would queue up to sell to you. Unfortunately, that is not true. The hard part about buying health insurance is getting the insurer to issue you a policy. Most insurers are risk-averse and would rather reject a healthy person than insure an unhealthy one. In one of the companies I worked for, the definition of superior performance was 'can leap over tall buildings in one bound'.[14] I had laughed out at the time. Unfortunately, the joke was on me, because insurers sometimes use a similar benchmark to select people to insure.

Consider some of the rejections I have seen over the past few months. A healthy person (to my untrained eye) disclosed in his health insurance application that he was anxious by nature. The insurer promptly declined the insurance and refused to conduct a medical test. A visitor to our website wrote about their autistic child. Insurers decline insurance for people with autism, even though autism is not a disease in the traditional sense. A sixty-year-old lady was declined insurance by three insurers because she complained of knee pain. A friend was turned down because he had lower-back pain even though he had a different insurance by the same insurer for over four years without making a single claim. A young boy who suffered burns because hot milk was spilt on him was turned down. That must have made his mother terribly angry.

If you have had kidney stones removed, many insurers will decline health insurance. Counterintuitively, your chances of being insured are higher if the kidney stones have not been removed! A man in his mid-fifties was turned down because he had been on mild medication for hypertension. Individuals suffering from multiple sclerosis or epilepsy struggle to buy insurance.

Regrettably, there is little public information on how many applications are declined by insurers but it is high, sometimes as much as 30 per cent. I estimate that over five lakh applications get rejected each year. Such a high decline rate creates many issues. The purchase process is frustrating because the effort of filling a form, paying and getting medically tested goes to waste.

Most just give up after the first rejection. Rejection leads to considerable anxiety. The worry is often unfounded because an insurer's view of health is more conservative than a doctor's.[15] The family physician will laugh away a problem that makes the insurance underwriter see apocalypse. The cost of rejection is borne by you, because medical fees are deducted from the premium refund. Finally, future applications require the buyer to declare that s/he was rejected, and this results in more rejection. It is a vicious cycle.

Insurers can underwrite more thoughtfully without increasing their risk. There are many examples to emulate—consider insurance for those who are HIV positive in South Africa. Over 15 per cent of South African adults are thought to be HIV positive and a few years ago over 40 per cent of deaths there were AIDS-related. Despite such a grave situation, insurers issue life and health insurance to HIV-positive buyers with no medical tests. Underwriters found that longevity and morbidity of HIV-positive people who take antiretroviral drugs regularly, is similar to the general population. So, their condition for issuing insurance is that the buyer must regularly take medication. This is monitored by lab reports and other declarations. Non-compliance with medical treatment results in the insurance lapsing. As expected, compliance rates are high. I was also struck by the fact that the proposal form for these insurances is just two to three pages. Similarly, in other markets, insurers issue health insurance to women with benign lumps in the breast because they get into the nature of the lump and its link to morbidity. Birth defects and neurological disorders also get covered.

Until we do more sophisticated underwriting, here is how to buy insurance if you suffer from a health condition. Select products where disclosures required are specific and not general. Consider this question in a stand-alone health insurer's proposal form: 'Within the last two years have you consulted a doctor or healthcare professional?' Avoid such broad questions because they put the onus on you to declare all medical ailments, even if you perceive them to be unimportant. Instead opt to fill out the form of a competing health insurer, who lists out specific diseases and asks if you suffer from those.

Do not add extra information. You need not confess to having been overweight a few years ago, or the fact that you smoked a cigarette once in high school. If you have a doubt, ask the insurer for an assessment of your application before formally applying. Some insurers will do this. That is an excellent option because a rejection does not become part of your permanent record and you may approach other insurers more willing to insure you.

Do make sure that you do not hide medical issues deliberately. Insurers will eventually find out and will not pay your claim, if the details hidden directly affect the claim.

Finally, you can buy top-up health insurance that has high deductibles. A deductible is the amount of a hospital bill that you must pay yourself before the insurance gets activated. In these plans a certain initial amount of the medical bill is paid by the patient and the remaining by the insurer. Because of this deductible, insurers will issue these insurances more readily.

A common pre-existing condition in India is diabetes. Can a diabetic be insured?

Can Diabetics Buy Insurance?[16]

A question I am often asked, particularly by senior citizens, is if diabetics can buy health and term insurance.[vi] They can, but

---

vi   Term insurance refers to an insurance product where no returns are given if you live through the insurance's tenure, but a large benefit is paid to your nominee if you die.

the buying process and product selection have to be carefully planned. The buying process is important because rejections by insurers become a part of your permanent record. Mis-declarations by you at this stage can later result in your claim being rejected. Delayed renewal (i.e., delays in payment of premium) can also lead to a significant loss in insurance benefits.

A few insurers provide a pre-formal application opinion. This they do by evaluating your previous medical records and letting you know the likelihood of your getting an insurance. Any feedback from them, at this stage, is informal and not part of your records. This means that when you apply to other insurers you need not state that your application was rejected by another insurer.

Give complete details of your diabetic condition in the proposal form, or to the medical underwriter. This prevents potential claims being rejected for medical non-disclosure. Finally, do not miss a renewal in your insurance. On both health and term-life, insurers cannot change the terms of insurance after you have bought it, unless you delay renewal. In health insurance a renewal lapse will lead to the waiting periods for diseases, including diabetes, being reset. In life insurance the insurer may decide not to reissue the term plan if your health has worsened.

Product selection depends upon your diabetic condition.

- **Gestational diabetes**: Developed during pregnancy, it often clears up over time. Insurers will issue standard covers to women even if they have had a prior gestational diabetes condition. You may need to wait for a few months after having a baby to purchase the insurance.
- **Type 1 diabetes**: This type is insulin dependent and difficult to insure. There are just a few options available. For instance,

you can be insured through a group cover if your company offers that as a benefit. To insure for death, you could opt for an individual personal accident insurance. Your nominee will be paid if you die because of an accident. Accident insurance is not dependent upon your health. Most general and health insurers offer personal accident insurances.

- **Type 2 diabetes**: In this case the body develops insulin resistance. It is the most usual form of diabetes and is easier to insure for. If diabetes onset is recent or the medication low, then most insurers will issue standard health- or term-insurance policies with a premium loading. The extent of premium loading is likely to vary between 10 and 30 per cent. These are the best products to buy because they are comprehensive. Health insurance, in particular, is renewable lifelong. When buying health insurance, do see that the insurer does not permanently exclude coverage for diabetic conditions. In term-life insurance, diabetes-related exclusions are not allowed. So, death as a result of diabetes will always be covered. In fact no health condition is excluded from coverage at any time. The only situation when a claim will not be paid is suicide in the first year of the policy.

If your diabetes is severe then insurers may not issue standard health or term insurance. In such situations you can buy diabetes-specific health plans. Such insurances cost about ₹20,000 for a ₹3 lakh cover. These plans also incentivize you to keep fit and measure sugar levels regularly. Very few plans cover both type 1 and type 2 diabetes.[17]

You may also want to enhance your cover, by buying disease-specific insurances such as cancer or dengue care.[18] These health insurances do not require medical tests and will be issued to you even if you have diabetes. These are a cost-effective way to enhance insurance. For life cover consider buying the personal accident insurance as previously described. The best safeguard, of course, is to buy your insurances early and take diligent care of yourself.

Insurers are good in dealing with physical illnesses such as diabetes and hypertension. But what about mental illnesses that have only increased during the pandemic?

Why Insurance Fails People With Mental Illness

Throughout my school and college years, Bai lived with us, moving across cities, helping us grow, for all practical purposes a dear family member. As she grew older, Bai began imagining that people were attacking her. We could not understand what had happened but ultimately, she went back to her village and died a few years later, untreated for schizophrenia.

Mental illnesses are prevalent, some consider it an epidemic, and this has only worsened during the pandemic. The challenges in addressing mental illness are considerable and include building awareness among patients and doctors, and building treatment capacity. Insurance currently plays a minor role in mental illness and we could do more.

The first issue is that people with mental illness find it difficult to buy health insurance, even if their conditions are minor. This leaves them uncovered even for physical illnesses. I have seen many insurance proposals rejected for conditions such as stress and anxiety, and proposals for more serious mental conditions get turned down immediately. So, most persons with mental health issues do not disclose their condition, which exposes their future claims to rejection. Some families with children that live with mental illnesses have health insurance because it was bought many years ago when the child's health condition was not asked for. Today that would be difficult.

The second issue is that the guidelines to underwrite insurance for persons with mental health issues are not explicit. In June 2020, IRDAI asked all insurers to upload their underwriting approaches for children that live with mental illnesses on their website by 1 October. The thought being that such persons or their guardians should know how insurers will treat their insurance application.

When I checked, only a handful of insurers had complied and the policies put up on the website were not meaningful. For example, insurers said they 'treated physical and mental illnesses at par. Like physical illnesses, mental illnesses would be subjected to evaluation and based on the outcome, each application would either be accepted as standard or with additional premium and/ or waiting periods, or rejected based on how chronic, severe it was, and what were the complications due to the disease or treatment.' The insurers also said that 'the acceptance of proposals with declaration of any conditions falling under the above mentioned categories would be as per the underwriting guidelines of the specific product and pre-policy medical tests.'

This is difficult to decipher, unhelpful to the public at large, and appears to be a declaration just to tick the regulatory box.

The third, more complex issue is to design products that cover the largely OPD-based treatment and caregiver costs of mental illnesses. Most health insurances cover hospitalization costs but these are relatively infrequent in mental illness. Treatment is mostly provided on OPD basis. Treatment sessions are expensive, because there are few specialized counsellors, psychologists and psychiatrists and each session can take a long time. A complete treatment cycle can cost between ₹10,000 and 20,000.

Caregiver cost is also high for the more advanced mental conditions. And often such care is needed lifelong. I vividly recall a panel discussion some years ago where a dignified gentleman in his eighties told me about his severely autistic daughter. He worried about who would look after the girl when he died and I had no answer. I certainly do not expect insurance to solve all these problems, but there must be ways that we can chip in more.

Insurers could be more open to selling health insurance to persons with minor, manageable illnesses. They could develop products or add-ons, priced to their satisfaction, specific to mental illness. Most importantly, insurers could consider building capacity for mental health issues and price this as a value-added service. Recently, we started a complimentary mental-health related OPD service for employees of our clients and a large number of people reach out to us every week. This can be done for mental health on a much larger scale by insurers. They could partner with mental health institutions to create capacity. Some, such as Sanjivini Society for Mental Health in Delhi, offer free and high-quality counselling and understand the issues and solutions deeply. Had Bai been diagnosed for schizophrenia, the cost of treatment to allow her a full, normal life would have been no more than a few hundred rupees in those days. This incident took place thirty-five years ago, but on mental health, time has stood still (even though costs have gone up).

If you or someone in your family suffers from mental illness then the best solution is to select an insurer whose proposal focuses on pre-existing physical ailments, declare the medication that you are taking fully and explain to the insurer that the mental ill-health need not translate into hospitalization later. In fact, this principle holds true for any pre-existing health issue that you have. The question is how much of your health condition to declare to the insurer and when?

Can Medical Over-Disclosure Be a Problem?

Some years ago, a middle-aged gentleman was recommended cataract surgery. He applied for a cashless claim. The family-floater health insurance that he was part of, had been running for five years and no claims had been made yet. The insurer, when assessing the claim, found out from the doctor's notes that the patient had been suffering from a medical condition called sleep apnoea over the past seven years and this fact had not been declared when the insurance was bought five years ago. The insurer rejected the claim and cancelled the family-floater (the entire family's insurance) on grounds of medical non-disclosure.

Non-disclosure of a pre-existing medical condition is one of the top three reasons for claim rejection. Such cases throw up several questions on the principles of health insurance. The first is, why does non-disclosure take place?

In most situations, medical non-disclosure is deliberate, with the salesperson and insurance buyer mutually deciding to hold back information. Their worry, not unfounded, is that if the health condition is transparently shared then the insurer will not provide insurance. In my own insurance buys, I have been guilty of nudging the nurses to add an extra inch or cut a few kilos so that my body mass index (BMI) falls squarely within the acceptable range. However, such behaviour simplistically assumes that insurers will not find out undisclosed information.

We significantly underestimate the insurer's strong capability to find out. When claims are filed many years after buying the insurance, customers always forget what they had disclosed in the proposal forms but insurers never do. They can access meticulously recorded diagnosis sheets and internal hospital case reports and get the facts fairly quickly. This is why, in addition to the obvious point that one should tell the truth, buyers should give accurate information and make sure this is properly recorded in the proposal form. When in doubt, disclose.

However, as mentioned earlier, you should watch out for very general catch-all medical questions in the proposal form. These are the questions that insurers ask so that you will declare anything of note that they may not have asked you already. Some of these catch-all questions encourage non-disclosure, because they are so broad in scope. Commonly posed questions ask if you have been under any regular medication (whether taken by your own decision or prescribed by a doctor), or undergone any hospitalization or illness or surgery. The answer to this is always going to be 'yes', which means that more detailed questions will follow.

That is why buyers expediently say 'no', resulting in possible non-disclosure which they may rue many years later when making a claim. A few insurers use more specific questions and will ask if you are currently suffering from any symptom(s) or complaint(s) persisting for more than five consecutive days. These can be answered more easily and you should prefer the products of such insurers, particularly if you do have a pre-existing ailment.

For a moment, let us assume that you have sinned and hidden a medical issue. Should that always be grounds for rejecting a claim or cancelling the insurance? I think not. Regulations require that the insurer ask itself what it would have done had it got that information earlier. If it would have issued the insurance, then the claim must be paid; but if the non-disclosure would have been grounds for rejecting the proposal then the insurer is right in rejecting the claim now. The problem is that these rules are not transparent and, at the time of a claim, insurers are most likely to argue that the non-disclosure was important enough for the claim to be rejected.

An important consideration is how many years after buying insurance is the claim being made. With regard to life insurance, the law specifies that claims cannot be rejected after three years.[19] In health insurance the regulations specify a look-back period of eight years after which a claim cannot be rejected.[20]

Let us now advance with the assumption that there was non-disclosure that was relevant and resulted in an early claim. Even in such situations the insurer should not unconditionally cancel the insurance if other family members are part of the plan. Why should they be left uncovered because one person in the family hid information? I have seen cases where such summary cancellation has taken place. In one case a spouse's claim was rejected on the grounds that the primary insured had hidden information. If you find yourself in this situation then do ask the insurer to penalize only the person who hid the information and not the other family members.

Finally, if the circumstances are such that the health insurance must be cancelled, then there is the matter of premiums paid. You will be refunded the premium for the unutilized time of the health insurance.

Returning to the case that I started out with. The insurer initially terminated the entire family's insurance but, through a process of grievance redressal, finally agreed to continue the family's insurance but not the person's who had hidden information. That was a good decision. What should you do if your claim was rejected because of medical non-disclosure?

Is Cold, Hard Logic or Emotion Better to Challenge a Claims Decision?

A frequent reason for rejecting health insurance claims is that the health condition existed before the insurance was bought.

Such pre-existing conditions are defined as illnesses for which there were symptoms or treatment up to four years before the buying of the insurance.[21] These pre-existing conditions are typically excluded in the early years of an insurance.

As mentioned above, pre-existing conditions are often an issue because they are not declared transparently when buying insurance. Buyers worry, and rightly so, that insurers will increase premiums or not issue a policy if they suffer from chronic or serious ailments. That is the reason many 'forget' to mention medication for hypertension or diabetes. One person vehemently argued with me that beta blockers were not medication. However, such buyers underestimate an insurer's tenacity. Insurers will get this information from doctors' prescriptions, discharge summaries, case notes, the hospital's internal daily reports, and independent investigations. You can run but not hide.

If your claim was correctly rejected, accept gracefully and move on. Writing to the CEO, the Board or the Prime Minister will not get your claim paid. However, if the claim was wrongly rejected, then fight it out. The most compelling way is to make a strong logical argument and ensure that someone senior reads your note.

Depending upon what the facts are, you could make one of these three arguments:

- **You did not know you had a prior illness:** Regulations require that you are aware you have had the disease; not just that the symptoms existed. This rationale can work for internal cysts, cancers, gynaecological conditions, kidney stones, liver-related issues and many more.
- **Your claim is not related to a pre-existing condition:** Illnesses can have many causes. If your doctor can explain

that there is a high possibility of the cause being something other than a pre-existing ailment, then the claim will be paid. Let us say that you did not disclose asthma but were later diagnosed with a heart condition. The insurer can say that because of this non-disclosure your claim is not payable. But if you demonstrate that the heart condition has nothing to do with asthma then the insurer may pay your claim. Another typical example is retinal degeneration that is often, but not always, caused by diabetes. Similarly, cirrhosis of the liver is not always the result of alcoholism.

- **The doctor certifies that you do not have a pre-existing disease:** A doctor's statement is given the most importance in a claim. A credible document that explains why the pre-existing ailment was mentioned in the medical history inadvertently, can convince insurers.

You should first write to the grievance officer at the insurer's office. If dissatisfied with the response then escalate the matter to the insurance regulator (IRDAI), or the Insurance Ombudsman.[vii] The IRDAI redirects complaints to the insurer and instructs them to relook at the matter. The Ombudsman will call the insurer and

---

vii   As per the IRDAI website:
The Insurance Ombudsman scheme was created by the Government of India for individual policyholders to have their complaints settled out of the courts system in a cost-effective, efficient and impartial way. There are at present seventeen Insurance Ombudsman in different locations and any person who has a grievance against an insurer, may themselves or through their legal heir, nominee or assignee, make a complaint in writing to the Insurance Ombudsman within whose territorial jurisdiction the branch or office of the insurer complained against, or the residential address or place of residence of the complainant is located. (https://www.policyholder.gov.in/ombudsman.aspx)

you for a hearing, typically after a few months, and then decide the case. Judgements are in favour of those claimants who have strong medical documentation and unambiguous evidence that information was not deliberately hidden.

You can, of course, obviate many of these issues by buying insurance with shorter waiting periods of two or three years before you can claim insurance for pre-existing conditions. Once these waiting periods are completed, the insurer cannot deny your claim. Persisting with the grievance redressal process can be daunting, like a David-and-Goliath battle. But do follow through consistently. David did finally win.[22]

The issues in claim settlement, however, are not always that of the insurer or buyer. In many cases hospitals fall short, and selecting the right doctor and hospital is as important as having the right insurance. How do you do that?

How Much Difference Can Selecting a Hospital Make?[23]

Health insurance and hospitals must both work when you fall ill. Over the years, there has been substantial improvement in health insurance. Minimum product standards have been set, definitions standardized and basic claims information made public. Buyers can make informed choices and switch insurances if they want.

Hospitals, though, have not kept up. The original Hippocratic oath and its modern versions that medical practitioners take while receiving their MBBS degree, are the finest documents on professional ethics. Some early versions had the promise of *nil nocere* or 'do no harm'. All versions speak of treating patients holistically. Yet there are several issues today that need to be addressed.

First, hospital incentives create a conflict of interest with patients. Some time ago, I had a backache and visited a doctor who recommended an MRI. He called the imaging centre and made the introduction. I paid an OPD fee of ₹700 and the MRI cost me ₹9,000. Diagnostic centres will often pay up to half the diagnostic cost to the referring hospital as a fee. In my case the MRI was needed, but a referral fee in general creates an incentive for expensive tests. Within hospitals, doctors are encouraged to prescribe tests. Diagnostic costs are borne by patients so they push back when costs are high. However, there is no such balance when insurance is available.

A poor lady I know was insured for ₹1 lakh. She went to the hospital for a cataract surgery that normally should have cost about ₹15,000, but was hospitalized because her blood sugar was high and her entire sum-assured of ₹1 lakh was used up. This patient was not informed when her insurance got over and ended up paying ₹30,000, her lifetime's savings, out-of-pocket. Many patients do not understand the nuances of insurance, and hospitals seek to increase costs when insurance is involved.

Getting into a hospital when you have insurance is easy. But getting out is not. The average discharge time for patients, after being declared fit, is over six hours.[24] A large part of this delay is because hospitals are bad at collating all the documents needed for cashless approval. Once, after waiting many hours for discharge, a friend threatened to walk out of the hospital but could not because the nurse refused to remove the cannula inserted in her vein, until the paperwork was done.

Billing practices in hospitals are flawed. To start with, initial deposits are taken from patients even if they are fully insured. Billing for the doctor's fees and the diagnostics vary by the type of room in which one is hospitalized. Patients in single rooms could end-up paying twice as much for tests, as those in wards. This is illogical because costs should not vary by room type.

The quality of a doctor's medical advice does not differ by a patient's wealth.

The fact that billing is based on the number of days a patient is hospitalized, also creates strong incentive to keep patients longer than necessary. Hospital bills can include charges, over and above customary hospital costs, for items such as toothpaste, weighing scales, bandages, linen and admission cards issued to relatives/guardians. Health insurance guidelines explicitly list 199 such items that are excluded from health insurance unless specifically approved.

The issue with such billing is that insurers are building sub-limits and exclusions into their products. For example, insurers cap claims based on room rent. Stay in a room twice as expensive as allowed by insurance, and you will get paid half the total medical bill. The IRDAI has sought to make this more rational by introducing a guideline on how deductions should be linked to room rent. Specifically, it prohibits indiscriminate reductions in a claim not linked to actual charges by the hospital.[25] A solution is to set more pre-determined package costs for specific ailments. In one sweep this removes all incentives for wasteful medical care.

How can you decide which doctor to visit? Several doctor discovery platforms have been developed but these provide only contact details and, in a few cases, subjective customer ratings. In the absence of good quality, publicly available information you will have to depend upon word of mouth and reputation. Seeking advice from a doctor about good hospitals to go to can be invaluable because you get an insider's perspective. Try to determine information such as the doctor's background, experience and outcomes to make an informed choice.

However, the patient-doctor trust has broken down to such an extent today that being a doctor is hazardous. Last year, I took someone who had got hurt on the head to the Casualty

OPD in a Delhi hospital. There was a prominently displayed warning that patients who manhandled doctors could be jailed. I waited as the patient was stitched up, a minor issue thankfully. The atmosphere was tense. One patient nearly slapped the receptionist because his name was not spelt right. A few minutes later several aggressive family members surrounded a doctor, questioning every step that he had taken.

The corporatization of hospitals has resulted in a clash between the patient-driven practice of medicine and profit-oriented approach of administration. Treatments are sometimes insurance-driven. Costs certainly are. A close friend had a minor day care ENT surgery. She was told that if she paid she would be charged ₹90,000 but if she claimed insurance the cost would be ₹2 lakh. That is a significant difference for no reason. Returning to the issue of my backache, the better solution, which I opted for, was a gradual, conservative physiotherapy but insurance would only pay for surgery.

To resolve these issues you need to appreciate that doctors also must earn an income and face many obstacles to their work. The medical fraternity, in turn, would do well to refresh its vows to the Hippocratic oath, a recent version of which cautions doctors against overtreatment.

Health insurance is one of the most important insurances that you will buy (term-life being another). However, it is not a panacea for all health issues. What are the current limitations of health insurance?

Understanding the Limitations of Health Insurance

A core principle that I was taught while building a career, was to always provide solutions when asked a question. Many years ago, in my first job at a fast-moving consumer goods (FMCG) company,[26] my boss and I would travel into the interiors of Andhra where he would ask me about the crops on the roadside, harvesting cycles, Telegu signposts, and erratic sales. I answered all his questions confidently, safe in the knowledge that neither of us knew the answers. Over the years, I like to believe, my solutions have become more fact-based.

Two incidents a couple of years ago reminded me that I do not always have all the answers and my field of work, insurance, has considerable limitations. I was invited to a panel discussion on mental health and insurance.[27] The audience consisted mostly of caregivers and some people suffering from mental illnesses. The panellists were from the insurance industry, NGOs and the medical profession. The most poignant question was from an eighty-year-old, ramrod-straight gentleman who said that he had taken care of his autistic daughter all his life, but, he asked, 'Is there an insurance that can take care of her after I die?' We, the panellists, spoke about risk, underwriting and products but the plain fact is that insurance cannot help in a situation such as his.

The second incident concerns a migrant family that I have known for a few years. A member of the family developed high fever and we directed him to a private hospital. Since hospitalization costs were high, about ₹30,000, he went to a nearby secondary-care government hospital. However, no beds were available and he was redirected to a premier tertiary-care government hospital. Here, he was admitted but had to sleep on the floor, due to lack of beds. After a day, worried about the poor hygiene, he decided to return home, suffered a relapse and died a few days later.

There are many situations such as these two, where insurance cannot help. People suffering from serious illnesses are the most eager to buy health insurance. But for most it is already too late. If you have had a disease that impacts one of the core body systems—cardiac, endocrine, psychological, neurological, renal amongst others—then it is difficult to buy any insurance at all. For people suffering from mental ill-health the issue is not so much that mental illness costs cannot be covered, but more that even their physical ailments are not insurable. You must buy health insurance when you are well and do not need it.

Similarly, insurance is ineffective if the main costs are for OPD medicines, diagnostic tests or home care. In the case of mental illnesses the caregiver's time is most expensive. In cases of strokes, hospitalization may not be extensive, but the primary cost for the patient is the loss of their ability to work and earn. In those COVID-19 cases which are not serious, the cost is of home quarantine, personal protection equipment (PPE) and diagnostic tests. In the case of drugs some, such as Diovan (that prevents the relapse of heart conditions), are not covered under insurance because they are preventive (and not curative) in nature. In the case of an organ transplant, the patient requires medication for extended periods, but these costs are excluded after the customary sixty days of post-hospitalization care. Similarly, dental treatment and cosmetic surgery are generally not insured.

Some newer insurance products can help but in a limited way. Over the years, critical-illness plans have steadily improved and now include diseases such as strokes, Alzheimer's and Parkinson's, that do not require hospitalization. Such insurances pay a fixed benefit not linked to actual medical costs. Similarly, some insurers have launched specific 'Corona Rakshak' insurances that also pay a fixed benefit.[28] Today, there are also a few products for people suffering from cancer, cardiac issues or diabetes; and at least three insurers will cover accidents during adventure sports, some will allow emergency treatment pertaining to pre-existing health conditions during overseas travel, and terrorist- and war-related risks can also be covered at a cost.[29]

As of now, insurance does not help in cases that require long-term care. The commonest afflictions of the elderly require high quality home care for life. Nurses or paramedics may be needed on call. In many situations assisted living is required. In some international markets, long-term care insurance has been introduced, rather unsuccessfully, because care costs are extremely high. These costs are hard to insure.

Insurance is not a substitute to building quality medical capacity. For the migrant that died, the issue was that both private and government hospitals failed to give him basic care in a hygienic or affordable manner. Understanding these limitations is the starting point to finding meaningful solutions.

Over time newer products and improvement are expanding the cover that health insurance can offer. One reason the scope of health insurance will rapidly increase is that the government is setting up its own schemes that offer comprehensive cover to the poor. This then sets a benchmark for what the industry ought to provide. The largest such scheme is the Ayushman Bharat National Health Protection Mission launched in 2018. What will be its impact?

How Can You Ensure that the Under-Privileged are Insured?

The Ayushman Bharat National Health Protection Mission (AB-NHPM) was launched in 2018. It gives ₹5 lakh of health cover to 500 million people for free. The scheme is still evolving. If successful, it will set several records in scale and quality of care. The deepest impact, however, will be the confidence it will instil in the poor. There are many workers and staff who are eligible for this scheme but not aware of it. You should encourage workers, domestic staff and other poor persons to check their eligibility. The scheme also impacts you positively because it sets a high benchmark for mediclaim insurances sold by insurers.

Under AB-NHPM, 40 per cent of the country's population will be insured immediately. The quality of healthcare that has been assured is excellent. Typically, schemes for the poor are watered-down versions of what paying customers get. In this case, though, the cover being offered is substantially superior to regular mediclaim insurance. The sum assured is more than what most paying customers personally own. The AB-NHPM scheme includes many items typically excluded in standard mediclaim: pre-existing diseases, mental health conditions, and internal congenital diseases, amongst others. If this scheme were to be compared with other health insurance products it would likely score an 'A'.

The product design is simple and easy to administer. Enrolment is automatic and no forms need to be filled. Entire families, irrespective of size and age, are covered. Eligible persons can walk into a hospital with their Aadhaar card and be treated. The network of hospitals being created is larger than what insurers have today. There are stringent service-level agreements: a pre-approval is required for all non-emergency cases, but if the request is not addressed within twelve hours then the treatment is considered approved. The treatment is cashless, which means that patients do not need to pay and can opt to be treated anywhere in the country.

Implementation at such a scale and with so many benefits is bound to face obstacles, the most substantial of which is the need for healthcare institutions to be economically sustainable. At the moment, hospitals are unhappy, because in their view, package rates fixed by the government are loss-making. For example, the proposed cost of a Coronary Artery Bypass Graft is about ₹90,000. The Central Government Health Scheme (CGHS) rate for a CABG in Delhi is over ₹110,000, while private hospitals routinely charge over ₹3 lakh for a CABG.

Insurers worry that they will be left out because states have the option to select a 'trust' model that does not require insurers to participate. In fact, this is the preferred model for many states. Where insurers participate, the auction may push premiums to unviable low levels. There have been news reports of a tender in Nagaland where the lowest bid was less than ₹500 per family. Other bids were over twice that.

The insurer model has an inbuilt conflict of interest. The organizational committees that will deal with grievances of hospitals and insurers, consist primarily of government representatives. Their chief focus will be to have patients' claims paid and they have little incentive to solve the problems of hospitals or insurers. The trust system, that does not use insurers, has a different problem. There is less restraint on claims payment. Also, states are notorious for delaying payments and hospitals are concerned about payment cycles. Such challenges are to be expected. Success will depend upon how quickly and comprehensively these are identified and addressed.

The benefits of getting the AB-NHPM right are huge. Hospitals will build considerable capacity to meet the demand for beds. There are about 1.5 million hospital beds in the country at present. These cannot support the 500 million people who will have insurance. As hospitals see an increasing patient inflow, they will build capacity.

The scheme encourages hospitals to maintain certain minimum standards. The compensation to hospitals is 10 per cent higher if they are accredited by the National Accreditation Board for Hospitals & Healthcare Providers (NABH), and a minimum technology standard has been specified for hospitals to be eligible for this scheme. The medical fraternity will be forced to present a stronger fact-based case to the government to increase pricing of treatment packages. Organizational capacity is being built at district and state levels, to oversee the programme. For insurers and third-party administrators (TPAs), this is a large new market that will open up.

The most meaningful impact, however, will be on the confidence of the poor and lower income groups who will have this insurance. Five years ago we had arranged insurance for a group of 1,000 daily-wage earners.[30] Each family in this group was given a cover of ₹1 lakh, much less than what the AB-NHPM offers today. To our surprise, claims in the first year were miniscule. On analysing we found that when these workers walked into a private hospital they were turned away at the reception desk because nobody believed they could pay. Gradually, though, the workers began to assert themselves and got treated. Today, the claim ratio with these workers runs at 100 per cent, as with any other group in the country. They now walk into hospitals confidently, ask to meet doctors and quickly get themselves back in shape for work. Imagine the empowerment if the experience of these 1,000 workers could be expanded nationwide.

The Lady with Parkinson's

A few years ago, as I was walking from my office to the local market for lunch, an elderly lady standing on the roadside started speaking to me. I assumed she was asking for money and quickened my pace. Fortunately, some sixth sense made me turn around and ask her what the matter was. I then saw that she had severe Parkinson's disease, her right arm was shaking uncontrollably. She asked for directions to a well-known homeopathic hospital in the area. As I opened up Google Maps to find the shortest walking route, we began talking. The lady had tried to get treated in government hospitals but was unable to get to the right doctors. She decided to try homeopathy because it seemed more accessible and affordable. Did she have insurance? I knew what her response would be. As the hospital was a twenty-minute walk away, I hailed a cycle-rickshaw to take her there.

I couldn't stop thinking about this incident. Why was this lady, obviously in her seventies, alone? Why did she not get care in the government hospital? Why could she not afford to go to a private hospital? Why was she not insured? I was dismayed that even if she were insured, Parkinson's costs, which are mostly OPD, would most likely be excluded from any insurance coverage. In any case, no scheme or insurer would cover her for the homeopathic treatment she was now seeking.

Each of these questions is substantial. The support system for the elderly is rapidly disintegrating. A survey by HelpAge India suggests that two-thirds of the elderly are financially dependent upon others. Ninety per cent feel that they are in poor health. A friend, who has spent two years building a community for the elderly, tells me that it is a mistake to focus on physical health. Emotional health is more important. The major issue that seniors face is that they do not feel useful, have little say in family matters, and are not respected. Statisticians say that India is a young country, unlike Europe or Japan, but there are more elderly people in India than in Japan. Overseas, the old have formed support communities that are powerful. The American Association of Retired Persons (AARP) has a membership base of over 35 million and revenues of over USD 1.5 billion. The revenue comes from manufacturers and service-providers seeking access to the market of retired persons. This revenue is used to take care of the group. If the lady with Parkinson's was in the US and was an AARP member, somebody would have accompanied her to the hospital.

Our government hospitals are in shambles. A doctor working at a leading government hospital in Delhi told me that for expensive medical consumables, such as cochlear implants, they approach charities for support because internal procurement is cumbersome. Once a year, I visit the All India Institute of Medical Sciences (AIIMS), Delhi for a retina check-up by a leading eye surgeon. I get to see him in reasonable time because I know someone who gets me preferential access. That is the only way I can bypass the crowds spilling onto the roads and the metro station outside the hospital. Smaller health centres suffer chronic shortage of staff and infrastructure. Consequently, seniors have to depend upon private hospitals and doctors. The same HelpAge report suggests that over 70 per cent of seniors in poor households depend upon private doctors. It is in this context that health insurance is so critical to our infrastructure and well-being.

The quality of our health insurance products has been steadily improving. The insurances available today have standard definitions. Restrictions, such as limits on costs of certain diseases, waiting periods and pre-existing disease exclusions, have come down. However, the focus has remained on hospitalization and allopathy. Many of the medical issues that Indians face do not fit into this construct, particularly for the elderly. Senior citizens list their most pressing issues as body pain, poor eyesight, hypertension, arthritis, and asthma. Most of these are outside the purview of regular health insurances. Other diseases, where treatment is mostly OPD-based—such as Parkinson's, Alzheimer's, strokes and mental illnesses—are also largely uncovered.

Cover for select traditional systems of medicine has been introduced, but it is more from a marketing standpoint than for actual use. Generally, the treatment is restricted in amount, or limited to hospitalization, in a few centres. Public data on claims under traditional treatment is not available, but is certain to be insignificant. There is a need to push development of health insurance with far widers cover across health systems.

Returning to the lady with Parkinson's. There is one bright spot to the story. As she was leaving, I took out some money to pay the rickshaw driver. She held me with her left, steady hand, blessed me for pointing her in the right direction but insisted she had the money to pay for herself. I wish we had more such fiercely independent people, working hard to improve their future against all odds.

2
Life

LIFE INSURANCE IS a deeply penetrated financial product in the country. Credit for this must go to the vast network of agents and bank branches. However, despite being widely prevalent, the purpose of life insurance is poorly understood. We buy life insurance for possible investment returns, saving towards a financial goal like education, or a child's wedding, but very seldom for financial security were the main income earner to die. The concept of 'term insurance' is recent. This is a product where no returns are given if you live through the insurance's tenure, but a large benefit is paid to your nominee if you die.

Many of you have shared your portfolios of individual insurances with me, perplexed to find out that you are locked-in or the returns are well below inflation or that the death benefit is minimal. These are the situations you or someone you know may have experienced:

- A senior executive shared his insurances with a wealth management firm and was aghast to learn that the expected returns were just 2 to 4 per cent, well below inflation and certainly less than what many other prudent investments could deliver.

- A friend living overseas shared details of an insurance that his father had bought. The salesperson, in this case from a bank, had promised him outsized returns of over 15 per cent. When this issue was escalated to the bank they showed a much more realistic sales illustration, signed and approved by my friend's father.

- An acquaintance needed money to tide over loss of income during the pandemic. When he asked his insurer for a refund, he got less than half the premiums he had paid.

- An acquaintance bought life insurance with a sum assured of ₹5 crore and paid premiums for fifteen years. In his sixteenth year he forgot to renew it and which is when he then succumbed to COVID-19. Now his family will not get a single rupee because of this slip-up.

- A college friend reached out because someone known to him had died and they had no records of the insurances that had been purchased. Unfortunately, there is no central repository of life insurances and reaching out separately to thirty life insurers, asking them whether a particular person is insured with them, is next to impossible.

- A senior citizen bought a unit-linked insurance plan (ULIP) and later found that he had opted for an aggressive equity fund. As the markets fell, he lost a chunk of his retirement savings.

This section describes how to avoid getting caught in these traps. I walk you through the journey of a life insurance, from buying, claiming, to closing. The cases I have described so far are purchases gone wrong. That is not always the case. There are several good outcomes as well:

- A young lady studying in college lost her father to COVID-19. The family was devasted. Fortunately, the father had a term-life insurance for ₹1.25 crore which was quickly paid by the insurer. This money has now been carefully invested to take care of the young lady's mother, who is a homemaker. As I write this, the family is still grieving but the financial security from the insurance payment was a relief.

- An executive in a multi-national company bought a term plan for ₹5 crore with his daughter as a nominee. He died in a freak accident. Fortunately the sum assured was paid within days. The daughter had wanted to study in the UK and this dream will still be fulfilled with the insurance money.

Buy life insurance thoughtfully. It can make a big difference to your family if you die prematurely.

The Document You Must Read as Though Your Life Depends On It

The life insurance illustration is a vital policyholder protection document. It is a cost-benefit table detailing premium and expected monetary benefits over time. Insurers must, by law, make you sign an illustration specific to your purchase and not a general document. The illustration forms part of the policy pack and I suggest that readers pull out their insurance policies now as they read this chapter. The language of illustrations is technical, and this primer will help you better understand what you have bought.[31]

The illustration is important for insurers because this is the basis on which reasonable customer expectations are set. These expectations are then built into product pricing. For policyholders, the document clarifies deliverables. An illustration has the following information:

- **Personal details and product features:** The illustration mentions your name, date of birth, product, premiums to be paid, rider details and sum assured. Make sure that these basics are correct. Insurers have unpaid claims, running into crores of rupees, because they do not have the correct contact details for customers. If there are discrepancies write to the insurer and have these corrected. In ULIPs there will be additional information on funds selected and reduction in yield.

- **Guaranteed benefits:** There is a tendency for salespersons to communicate expected returns as guaranteed. Sellers may show an illustration and assure you that the amounts written will definitely be paid. That is why the regulator had a column for guaranteed benefits explicitly carved out. The ULIPs may not have any guarantees, in which case this section will be excluded. The illustration will list three guaranteed benefits:

  On maturity. This is the amount that you will be paid when the insurance completes its term. It does not depend upon interest rates or company performance.

  On death. The death benefit is different from the maturity amount. This is the amount that will be paid to your nominee if you die. The nominee will be the legal heir you have named in the insurance. However, if you have not named a nominee then all your legal heirs will have a claim on the insurance.

On surrender. Surrender is when you close the insurance mid-term. The amount paid to you has a penalty built in. The penalty is similar to the cancellation fee in an airline ticket. It can be quite high. The penalty depends on the insurance you purchased and the number of years you have had the insurance. The longer you remain in the insurance the lesser the penalty. The surrender amount mentioned in the guaranteed section is the minimum that you will get.

- **Illustrated scenarios at 4 and 8 per cent investment return:** An important driver of your insurance's performance is the return earned by the assets that the insurer invests in. A higher investment return will translate into more benefits for policyholders. However, the illustration can only show expected returns. To prevent irrational projections the regulator has specified that two scenarios must be presented, at 4 and 8 per cent. An insurer can illustrate at lower rates than this but not higher. An important, less understood, aspect is that the 4 and 8 per cent returns refer to an insurer's earnings. Policyholders get less because the insurer deducts costs.

This concept is true of all life insurances, but is explicitly called out in ULIPs where the illustration has an item called 'reduction in yield'. This reduction is capped by regulation and indicates how much less than the insurer's returns you will get. The smaller the reduction in yield, the better. Illustrations for ULIPs show the various charges that are deducted from your funds. You need not look at each of these individually because they are all captured in the overall reduction-in-yield number.

Each of these investment return scenarios has information on bonuses, maturity amount and death benefit. A special surrender value is listed. If you close insurance mid-term then you will be paid whichever is higher—the special surrender value or guaranteed surrender value.

To understand your actual returns in a traditional participating insurance, where bonuses are declared, you will need to pull out all the annual cashflows, both premiums paid and money received, from the illustration into an excel sheet and use the Internal Rate of Return (IRR) function to estimate the annualized returns. These tend to be between 3 and 6 per cent per annum for these insurances. These returns are not guaranteed but depend upon the performance of your insurer in terms of managing their costs and investment returns. You can also request your adviser to do this calculation for you since they are well-versed in the process. A projected IRR of over 8 per cent is not possible under the current regulations.

Do also make sure that the illustration in the policy document is what you had originally signed. Spending ten minutes on this document will give a clear view on your life insurance and prevent surprises.

The initial paperwork to be done in buying life insurance can be cumbersome. There will be a proposal form to fill, illustrations to review, tax returns to submit, and medical tests as well. You may want to simplify this by opting for insurances that have minimal paperwork. That is a mistake. Read on to know why.

Why 'Hassle-Free' and 'Quick-Issue' Insurances Can Be a Problem

I learnt the hard way that life insurance is a product that everybody needs but nobody wants. Twenty-seven years ago, when I began my career in a consumer goods company, I was astonished at the pace at which high-end cosmetics flew off retailer shelves. Here was a product that, in my simplistic view, nobody needed but everybody wanted. Ten years later, when I moved into insurance, I expected it to be easier to sell than consumer goods, because of the fundamental need for insurance. How wrong I was. Insurers struggle to get people to think about insurance. Even if people decide to buy insurance, less than half actually do.

Why is the drop-out rate so high? A major reason is the paperwork and complex process of buying insurance. Consider this, a standard proposal form requires you to furnish over a hundred bits of information about yourself; provide a self-attested identity, address and income proof; and perhaps undergo medical tests. All this needs to be done in physical format and documents typically move between insurer and customer several times. This process is called full underwriting and takes a few weeks. Several customers get frustrated with the complicated process and just drop out.[32]

Some years ago, insurers began to address this by introducing simplified-issue products. These are marketed as 'hassle-free', 'no-medical', 'Saral' or 'Tatkal'. These products have: (i) simpler proposal forms, (ii) no medical tests, and (iii) issuance in one go. They have become particularly popular in remote areas, smaller towns, with third-party distribution networks and the banking channels. Prima facie this seems a good development for people buying insurance but it really is not. Here is why:

- **Simplified-issue life insurance is expensive**: Life-insurance pricing is based on standard mortality rates. These rates are publicly available death rates based on a very large sample of people. All insurers use these rates as a base for pricing their insurances. A standard insurance product that goes through a full underwriting process and requires medical tests, will typically be priced at 70 to 80 per cent of the standard mortality rates. When you have undergone medical tests, the insurer has in-depth information on your health and can give you lower prices that accurately reflect your good health. Simplified-issue products get priced much higher—at 120 to 150 per cent of the standard mortality rates because insurers do not have sufficient information on your health. So, they assume that you are relatively unhealthy. Looked at another way, you may pay almost twice as much for the mortality or death benefit in a simplified-issue product, as compared to a fully-underwritten one. With one insurer, the cost of insurance increases from ₹10,000–17,000 per year for a forty-four-year-old person purchasing ten-year insurance with a ₹30 lakh sum assured. What this also means is that by buying simplified-issue products, healthy people subsidize the unhealthy. This is not a good insurance principle.

- **Simplified-issue products typically restrict the amount of insurance you can buy:** Insurers restrict their risk in simplified-issue insurance by specifying the limits of the maximum sum assured. The upper limit of this insurance ranges from ₹10–25 lakh. I recommend a death benefit that is ten-times your annual income, which means that these products are adequate for people earning less than ₹1–2.5 lakh a year. That is too low. Even if these insurances are bought from an investment perspective the returns will be lower than other products, because charges and expenses are higher. When simplified-issue products were initially introduced, they sometimes did not pay a death benefit in the first two or three years. This meant that in case of early death, only the premiums would be returned but the sum assured would not be paid. To IRDAI's credit, this concept of a death lien was removed because it considerably reduced the effectiveness of insurance.[33]

- **Medical questions are vague and leave room for claim repudiation:** A typical medical question in a simplified-issue insurance form is, 'Apart from minor ailments, such as cold and flu, have you received any treatment from any doctor or specialist or been hospitalized or undergone hospital treatment, in the last five years?' What is a minor ailment? Everybody I know has gone to a doctor in the past five years and should be answering yes to this question. In reality everybody answers no.

Including such questions allows the insurer to issue your policy without a medical test, because they know that if a claim were to be made they have the room to investigate and can then push back if needed. I am not suggesting that insurers will wilfully deny a legitimate claim in simplified-issue insurance. However, insurers are big organizations and I do see frontline claims executives exercising their own (sometimes incorrect) judgement in claims. It takes considerable effort to reverse those decisions.

Years ago, while travelling the mountain roads in Kashmir, I read a beautiful signpost put up by the brave engineers who risked their lives building those precarious roads. It said, 'When you go home tell them of us. Say that for your tomorrow we gave our today.' I am certainly not asking you to make that severe a sacrifice, but I do strongly recommend that you put in the considerable effort required today to buy a 'hassle-filled', 'medicals-included', fully underwritten life insurance product. It is a lot of hard work but will ensure that your nominees get the benefits you intended for them.

The best benefits that you can leave behind if you die, are from a term insurance. Yet, many hesitate to buy this. Why?

The 'Must-Have' Life Insurance Is the Hardest to Buy

Term-life insurance is a difficult concept. There are no returns if you live, but a large payment to the family if you die. Term-life accounts for less than 10 per cent of sales in India compared to over 35 per cent in the US. Apart from being an excellent insurance product, term insurance sales are the finest indicator of the life insurance industry's maturity. A high proportion of such sales indicates that the sales force is sophisticated enough to explain this difficult concept. If many buyers purchase term insurance it shows they understand the value of life insurance.

There are two obstacles to overcome when selling term cover. First, insurers must get better at underwriting. That is the process by which an insurer assesses an application, decides whether to issue the insurance and sets price. The rigid underwriting that life insurers follow results in several good applications being declined. Second, customer and intermediary fraud must reduce.

- A rich businessman applied for a term cover of ₹30 crore. The proposal was rejected because he had travelled to Côte d'Ivoire and Ghana some years ago. For some reason this was considered risky. I argued the case: It was just a two-day visit; he would never go there again; crossing the road in Delhi was just as risky; these countries played better football than India. The insurer firmly rejected the case.
- A thirty-five-year-old bought term insurance a few years ago for a premium of ₹8 lakh. Later that year the same insurer introduced a cheaper term plan that would have cost

this gentleman ₹5 lakh. A neat saving of ₹3 lakh. The person applied to the insurer to cancel the initial policy and purchase a new one. I was horrified when the insurer refused to accept his application, because the IT system did not allow for a term policy to be cancelled. It was the old expensive insurance or nothing at all. I escalated this to the CEO who allowed the application. During this fracas the person was temporarily uninsured, because his old insurance had lapsed and the new one was yet to be issued. Fortunately, the person did not die before the new term plan was issued.

- An entrepreneur who has set up a successful chain of speciality restaurants was denied a cover of ₹3 crore because his salary was low. But what of the significant business value that the entrepreneur had created and owned?

- A former colleague set up a ₹100-crore fund to invest in start-ups. The insurer was willing to insure the founders of the companies the fund invested in, but not the investor.

It takes so much effort to pursue these cases that most buyers give up. Why do insurers shy away from non-standard risks? There is a sameness to underwriting term insurance across insurers. If your application is rejected by one insurer you can be certain that others will have the same response. This is because most risks are reinsured[viii] with a handful of reinsurers who set prices

---

viii   A reinsurer is a company that insures the insurers. Insurers also pay a premium to reinsurers. In return, reinsurers will pay a large part of claims that the insurer is required to settle. This is called reinsurance. Reinsurers tend to be very big companies, operating globally, that have the financial strength to pay large claims. This system ensures the financial stability of insurers, particularly when there is a catastrophe with many claims. Reinsurers actively approve products that are introduced by insurers.

and drive underwriting. Effectively, there are not twenty-four insurers competing, for instance, but five reinsurers.

Developed markets are different. Insurers retain more risk and compete on underwriting. An insurer's preferences are known and drive business. One insurer has lower rates for smokers, another will underwrite hypertensives and yet another will issue insurance to people in disaster-prone areas. In one case a US insurer gave preferred rates to cigar smokers because these smokers were wealthy with access to quality healthcare.

Fraud is a big issue. In many cases intermediaries urge the buyer to hide information saying they will 'take care' of the claim. It does not work. Claims, where all the required information is not disclosed, are not paid. Buyers are also to blame. A senior executive in his application wrote that he did not smoke. Wisely, the insurer did a cotinine test and found nicotine. I asked the buyer why he lied and was told that a couple of cigarettes a day was not considered smoking. At least in Europe. In this case the insurer gracefully agreed to issue the insurance at higher smoker rates.

In 2019 there were fifty-six death-claim related complaints filed with the Insurance Ombudsman. Over fifteen of these were dismissed because the applicant had withheld relevant facts.[34] It is astonishing that a buyer will commit fraud and then actually appeal for justice! Fraud reduces over time as insurers emphasize upfront underwriting rather than investigations at the claims stage. Over time buyers realize that hiding relevant information harms them because their claims do not get paid.

Insurers must look at fellow general insurers to see how they have grown health and personal accident insurance. The key to market development has been a vibrant corporate business and a flexible underwriting approach that considers inputs from buyers and intermediaries. Life insurers should inculcate these.

Five years ago, the largest US term insurance distributor visited India to see if he could build a similar business here.[35] I was disappointed to see him conclude that the market was not ready. That should change now. It is about time we pressed forward on this important life insurance product.

Let us say you do go ahead and buy insurance. What happens if you need to surrender that insurance for whatever reason? Perhaps you need some money or you realized the insurance does not meet your requirement? How do you go about that?

The High Costs of Surrendering Your Insurance

I am often asked whether or not to surrender an insurance policy. Surrendering means to stop an insurance mid-term. The question is most difficult to answer in traditional life insurance because the analysis must factor in the downside of a surrender—penalty, taxes not being returned and loss of death benefit—against the possible benefit of better investment returns.

All insurances—life, general and health—have a provision for surrender if you have not made a claim. This provision is poorly understood because when you buy insurance the focus is on benefits and claim settlement. We do not expect to surrender insurance mid-term. However, circumstances do change, new products do get introduced or you may conclude that you bought the wrong insurance. Surrender is frustrating because you feel the pinch of penalties.

All insurance products allow early closures. In the free-look period, typically the first fifteen days after you receive the insurance, you can claim a complete refund. There may be some minor deductions for administrative or risk-related costs. This free-look period is allowed in life, health and some general insurances; and the clock starts from when you receive the insurance contract. So, the first thing to do when the documents reach you is to read them and decide whether this is what you wanted.

Surrender costs increase dramatically once the free-look period is over:

- **In health insurance** early exits are possible, but refunds are made using the short-period scale. This imposes a severe penalty—if you leave in the first three months 50 per cent of your premium will be refunded; between three and six months 25 per cent will be returned; and after six months nothing. These are the minimum amounts that need to be returned, but a few insurers pay more than the minimum scale.
- **In travel insurance** refunds are linked to the trip's start date. You can claim a full refund with minor deductions for administrative charges, if your trip is cancelled. You can also claim a deduction if you come back from the trip early. The rules vary by insurer but generally if you spend half the time you had planned for, you can get 25 per cent of your premium back.
- **In motor insurance,** similar to health insurance, surrender costs are decided according to the short-period scale.
- **In ULIPs** there are two distinct kinds of surrender periods:

  During the first five years you do not get your money back. On surrender the insurer will move your balance, after deducting the allowed charges, to a discontinuation fund where you earn 4 per cent return and this will be paid to you after five years.[36] The amount of the discontinuation charges allowed, is specified in the regulations.[37]

  If you surrender your insurance after five years then you may withdraw your accumulated funds without a charge.

- **In traditional life insurance** the surrender terms are more onerous. In these, no money is refunded if you close the insurance in the first year; 30 per cent of premiums paid are refunded in the second year; 35 per cent in the third year; 50 per cent in years four to seven; and 90 per cent is returned in the last two years.[38]

In all these cases, the act of surrender destroys value because you do not even get your capital back. This surrender scale is the minimum prescribed, and policyholder-focused insurers do pay more.

Surrendering an insurance is cumbersome, because of the processes. Life insurers often require that you visit the insurer's branch with the original policy copy. In health and travel insurance the process is simpler and may be done over email.

Insurers insist on a physical meeting before accepting a surrender because they would like to convince you to retain the insurance. They also try to determine if you are being incorrectly pushed into this decision by an adviser who seeks to make you replace your insurance with the objective of earning new business incentives.

You should consider surrendering an insurance policy only if you really need the money, or if the one you bought is completely different from what you expected. But once you have made the decision to surrender, see it through. I often see policyholders do a detailed analysis that suggests surrender is the best option for them. Yet they do not follow through with this because surrender is an explicit recognition that they made a judgement error. Vanity triumphs over practicality.

3

Pension

PENSION IS THE opposite of life insurance. Life insurance is meant to address the risk of dying early, whereas pension mitigates the risk of running out of savings if you are blessed with a long life. The chances of this happening are greater than people imagine. What if you have no money at a late age, say after eighty. Would you depend upon your children to take care of you? Do you have caregivers? This is not something you can take for granted.

Civil servants and service personnel earn attractive pensions after retirement. The pension amounts are linked to their last-drawn salary. However, the rest of us do not have this facility and it is up to us to make sure that our savings do not ever run out, so that we can live independently throughout our lives.

Much too often I see the elderly in distress on financial matters:

- An uncle transferred all his property to his children, secure in his expectation that they would care for him. That did not happen and eventually he had to live a simpler, more basic lifestyle. Had he sold or rented out his home, he would not have needed to make such compromises.

- An elderly relative invested his savings in an initial public offering (IPO) of a company's stocks, looking for quick returns. Unfortunately, the stock is now listed well below the purchase price and the relative has wiped out a large amount of his savings.

- An executive in his forties reached out. He wanted to withdraw the maturity amount in his pension plan, only to be told that the money had to be reinvested into an annuity and could not be withdrawn.

- At my wife's eye clinic she often sees elderly homemakers who have had poor vision for years. A ₹12,000 cataract surgery would have given them a much better quality of life, but the family would not make that investment.

This section describes why you need a pension and your options to buy a pension plan. You will understand the specific product features that pension plans have and will get acquainted with typical retirement issues. Knowing the issues and facing them squarely will help you avoid the most common pitfalls of retirement. With careful planning you could live a comfortable life, just like the happy seniors that show up in many insurance advertisements.

Can Longevity Be a Problem?

There are three distinct risks we face when growing old— dying early when your family is financially dependent upon you, illness, or dying at a very old age when you've run out of savings. Dying early, or suffering from ill-health are risks well understood and can be insured through life and health insurance. The risk of living too long is less obvious, which is why elders so often bless you to live to be a hundred.

The main risk in a long life is that you will run out of savings. This is difficult to predict because the event is so far ahead in time and many of the variables that determine future savings are not in your control. One such variable is inflation. Your effective return is what you earn on investments less inflation. Over the past two decades, the increase in the consumer price index, an indicator of inflation, has been between 2.5 per cent and 12 per cent per annum. Over the past few years, the average has been closer to 7 per cent. This eats into your savings.

Another important determinant of future funds is the interest earned. For example, if you leave your money in a savings account then your returns, on average, will be less than 3 per cent. If you invest in fixed deposits, then the rates would vary between 4.75 and 9.25 per cent.[ix] In several instances over the past two decades, your net earnings, which is interest less inflation, would have been negative or extremely low. In such a case, when you live long, the risk is that one day your savings get wiped out.

Good retirement planning addresses this risk by factoring in two stages: fund accumulation and annuity. Fund accumulation is the process of building up your savings, whereas annuity is the process of drawing down.[x] Fund accumulation can be

---

ix   This is the range of fixed deposit returns over the past twenty years for investment terms of one year or less.

x   In an annuity you make an upfront, one-time investment and then the annuity periodically pays you a fixed amount. If this fixed amount is more than the interest earned on your corpus then the initial investment you made gradually reduces. This is called a drawdown. The benefit of an annuity is that even if the corpus reduces to zero the insurer will still keep paying the regular payment that they have committed to.

done through many products such as the public provident fund, national pension scheme, insurance savings plans and mutual funds. However, the annuities are offered only by life insurers. Life insurers sell pension products that combine fund accumulation and annuity.

The main decisions when buying a pension plan, offered by life insurers, concerns the vesting age, premium payment term, investment preferences and type of annuity. The vesting age should be your expected retirement age, generally over fifty. If you are a salaried person, then buy an annual premium payment policy. If you have surplus investible funds then buy a single premium because those turn out to be more cost-effective. The investment decision depends upon your financial situation. Investment in government securities is safer, but has lower expected returns. Investing in equities (i.e., buying shares in a company) is likely to have higher returns in the long term, but is considerably more volatile. Government securities can be accessed through traditional, participating pension plans whereas equity through ULIPs.

There are several annuity options. The most popular is where an annuity is paid throughout your life and then the total premium returned to your nominee when you die. There are variants that do not pay capital back on death, but offer higher living benefits. It is also possible to buy joint life, fixed increase, or limited pay annuities.

There are some issues with pension plans that you must be aware of. First, at the end of the accumulation stage, pension plans allow you to withdraw only up to 60 per cent of the accumulated amount tax free. The remaining 40 per cent must be invested into an annuity.[39] This is a limitation because you commit yourself to an annuity many years before you will actually make the purchase. This also means that there is little flexibility to withdraw money if you have a financial emergency.

The other issue with pension plans is that annuities are taxed. This reduces the already modest returns. At age sixty, the implicit interest rate in an annuity is less than 7 per cent per annum. If this is taxed, at even 20 per cent, the returns are a relatively low 5.6 per cent, which are insufficient to create a real income after adjusting for inflation.

Watch out for a common mis-selling issue, which is to push pension instead of life insurance. Pension is much easier to sell because there are no medical tests, policy issuance is simple, and in the initial fund-accumulation stage both products look similar. The benefit of pension plans is that they force you to save for retirement.

These plans would be far more effective if: (i) insurers developed the ability to issue annuities that promise a real return after adjusting for inflation (ii) the government were to make annuities tax-free and (iii) insurers were to allow cash withdrawal in emergencies. Perhaps the next time someone wishes that you live to be a hundred, you may add the caveat 'with low inflation and high returns'.

Even though pension plans are necessary to plan your retirement they have made limited headway. Why?

Think Twice Before Buying an Annuity

As a young boy I would often accompany my grandfather to visit relatives in a colony built by the Delhi Development Authority (DDA). On one such visit I saw an old man sleeping on a cot out on the road. The bed was chained to a gate. I later learnt that the man's family had thrown him out of the house and he was forced to spend all his time on that bed. The situation is even more dire for women. Recently a group of Air Force wives in Gurugram sponsored an eye camp where an elderly lady was diagnosed with cataracts in both eyes. Her children, despite being relatively well-off, refused to pay for her surgery—a total cost of ₹12,000. According to the National Sample Survey 2004, over 70 per cent of such elderly women are fully dependent on others. How tragic.

Every management report underscores that India is relatively young. The average age in India is far less than the US, Japan or Europe. However, simply because we have a higher proportion of younger people does not mean that we have a small number of old people. According to the Census 2011, there are about a 100 million Indians who are over sixty years old. That is more elderly people than any of the countries mentioned here. The needs of the old are diverse, but my focus is on income and health because these are areas that insurance can address. But, unfortunately, does not.

An essential insurance to guarantee old age income is the immediate annuity. In this a person makes one payment in return for a lifetime of assured income. The lifetime income can be structured in many ways. Sometimes, the guarantee extends only for a few years, often the capital is returned when the person dies. The most important structure, however, is to guarantee an income for as long as the person lives. That is true insurance at work, because it caters to the financial needs of a really long life. In India, if one were to invest ₹50 lakh in an immediate annuity at the age of sixty, it would earn about ₹40,000 per month. That is a shade over 9 per cent per annum, not much more than what a fixed deposit pays senior citizens. To make matters worse, unlike a fixed deposit, no capital is returned to your nominee if you die. The final nail in the coffin (no pun intended) is that annuity income is taxed. That is why we do not see people queueing up to buy annuities.

In the US a comparable annuity pays 5 to 6 per cent per year, which is about five times the rate given by a fixed deposit. Do the US and other developed markets have a magic wand that allows them to pay so much more? No. It boils down to pure economics and we can learn from that. Insurers aggressively sell annuities because these counterbalance insurance risk—the risk (for an insurer) of an insured person dying early, is hedged by the risk (for the same insurer) of the person living too long.

Developed markets have a transparent and efficient market-mechanism to buy and sell long-term pension risks. Finally, governments and the private sector actively promote long-term bonds with high yields. Consequently, there are several interesting annuity options that have emerged. The ULIP annuities with guarantees have grown rapidly. A cost-effective product called the 'advanced life deferred annuity' also has potential. It provides an annuity only if one lives beyond a certain age. For example, it can be bought at sixty but will pay a monthly income only after you turn eighty-five. People with ill health can purchase 'impaired annuities' that pay them more since life expectancy is less.

The point is that there is far more product sophistication that insurers can bring into the market. There are other solutions to increasing income, such as increasing the retirement age for one. In both the private sector and government the effective retirement age is lower than sixty. We need to create jobs and capabilities that can keep people productive for much longer.

Another frequent problem is that several elderly Indians are asset-rich but cash-poor. Homes that the elderly own are valuable, but there is no way to monetize that asset. Some years ago companies introduced reverse mortgage loans and reverse mortgage loan-enabled annuities. These ideas have gained popularity in Europe and the US. The concept is that the elderly mortgage their home and earn a steady annual income. The person can continue living in the house until they die, at which time the house gets transferred to the bank.

Theoretically, this is an excellent idea that provides immediate liquidity. Practically the plans are riddled with operational issues and are a failure. For example, some reverse mortgage designs stop monthly payments after twenty years. Heaven help you if you live beyond twenty years. Another version includes provisions where the pay-out could change if the home's value fluctuates. To get the reverse mortgage product right would require real estate, insurance and banks to work together. It is an effort worth making.

In health the problem is that many diseases suffered by the elderly are not covered by insurance. Also, the limited insurance available is prohibitively expensive. Consider the facts—according to the *Situational Analyses of the Elderly in India, 2011* published by the Central Statistics Office, nearly one-third of the elderly reported an illness. The most common chronic diseases are related to the heart, urinary tract, diabetes, hypertension, joints and ulcers—broadly in that order. Treatment for most of these is home-based, requires nursing care and not hospitalization. This means that regular health insurance does not cover these treatments. Further, about six elderly people in every hundred suffer at least one disability. These disabilities are also not insured in a mediclaim. Alzheimer's and other mental diseases are spreading rapidly but are generally excluded from insurance unless they require hospitalization.[40]

Health insurance rates shoot up when you cross sixty. One of the A-rated health insurances in our mediclaim ratings, costs ₹9,800 for ₹5 lakh cover at age fifty. The premium increases to

₹29,000 after sixty-five. The solution is to increase the number of senior citizens buying health insurance. This will lower costs as the risk gets spread more widely. One idea is to mandate a portion of pension be used for health insurance. Also, insurers should consider introducing long-term care insurance. These pay for nursing care and assistance that the elderly need for basic acts of daily living. In Germany, buying long-term care insurance is mandatory.

We must take care of the old. After all, we will also get there one day. Bob Dylan, the poet, beautifully expressed this in his words: '[a]s the present now will later be past/. . ./And the first one now will later be last.' Finally, on a positive note, the old lady in need of cataract surgery in both eyes got it done. An NRI stepped up to pay for her.

4
Property

THE MOST VALUABLE asset for most is their home, whether bought or inherited. Despite the home's importance, it is seldom insured. I suspect this is because the frequency of property damage is low. Perhaps one in a thousand homes is damaged in any given year. The risk seems distant. But what we do not comprehend is that although the frequency is low, the cost of damage can be exceptionally high. Sometimes large enough to diminish the value of this asset materially. Consider these cases:

- A bungalow in Delhi had a basement where there was extensive seepage. It took days of work to identify the source of the water leak, which was on the first floor. This floor had to be vacated for a few days as repair was carried out. The final bill was ₹2 lakh.

- The electric wiring outside a house short-circuited and caught fire at night. The police and local electricians quickly came in and helped douse the fire, but the entire staircase was gutted. Over the next few days, a new panel had to be made, relocated outside the stairs and new miniature circuit breaker (MCB) boxes installed. The total cost was ₹90,000.

- The walls in the third-floor apartment of a multi-storeyed building developed cracks. The fourth and top floor had to be abandoned because the third-floor owners lived overseas and would not get the repair work done. As a result of this situation the top floor became unsaleable. The cost of the top-floor apartment was ₹3 crore.

- A well-known museum caught fire and was completely razed. What was worse, most of the artifacts inside were also destroyed. The artifacts were irreplaceable and the museum will need to be rebuilt from scratch.

- While building an extension to a balcony, a heavy metal grid fell and damaged the neighbour's house. A war of words ensued, with the police being called in. Finally, the neighbour had to be compensated ₹50,000 and a metal scaffolding that cost ₹30,000, was put up.

- Some burglars threw a stone at an apartment. The glass doors, made of sheet glass, broke. All the jewellery and paintings in the home were stolen. The total loss filed with the police was ₹15 lakh.

- The basement of a building was damaged during a moderate earthquake of about 5 on the Richter scale. The office in the basement had to move to a new location until the repair work was done. The cost of repair and renting new premises was about ₹5 lakh for a six-month period.

Insuring your home is simple and inexpensive. It takes years to build or acquire a home but just a few hours for it to be seriously damaged. A small investment in home insurance can protect you from large financial damages. This section explains how to go about this poorly understood but important insurance.

What Matters in a Home Insurance?

A friend owns a home in South Delhi for which she regularly paid insurance charges to the maintenance agency. Unfortunately, her home was gutted by fire. The insurance claim of ₹20 lakh was denied on two counts: (i) the insurance had been bought by the maintenance agency, which had no insurable interest in the property; and in any case, (ii) the home had been vacant for a few months.

Although home insurance has been around for years, it is not well understood by homeowners, agents and, I daresay, insurance salespersons themselves. The number of home insurances sold and claims paid is small. This will change. I have seen more interest in home insurance over the past year than in the past ten years. Some years ago, the devastating Nepal-centred earthquakes that shook many areas in India were a turning point. More recently, during the pandemic and fuelled by WhatsApp forwards, many feared that a large earthquake was imminent. This may not have a scientific basis but home insurance is once again a strong need. A home is the most significant asset that people own—that is why insuring it is important, next only to buying term and health insurance.

The four considerations when buying home insurance are: determining the sum assured, setting the basis on which damage will be valued, buying relevant extensions and being aware of the warranties.

The sum assured is set at the value of the property, should it be destroyed. The norm is to consider total cost of construction and exclude land cost. So, for a given quality of construction it does not make a difference where your home is located.

Most struggle with this concept because in their minds the home is worth crores whereas the construction cost insured is in lakhs. A rule of thumb for high quality construction is ₹4,000 to ₹5,000 per square foot. Buyers need to be careful about under-insurance. In other words, if you insure your home for less than the cost of construction, then any claim paid will be proportionately reduced. For example, if the actual construction cost is ₹50 lakh but you buy insurance for ₹25 lakh, then for any future claim you receive you will be paid only half. So, for example, if you have a fire that costs ₹10 lakh to repair you will be paid only ₹5 lakh.

The basis on which damage is valued is key. This can be on the basis of the market value, reinstatement value, or agreed value:

- **Market value** is a misnomer; it actually refers to only the depreciated value being paid. For example, let us say you have a wooden cupboard that cost ₹20,000 to make. If this cupboard is damaged five years later, you will be entitled to about half the cost, ₹10,000. This comes as a surprise to homeowners.
- **Reinstatement value** refers to paying you the cost of replacing a damaged item with a new one, or the cost of repairs so that the damaged item is 'like new' again.
- **Agreed value** means you propose the value, and the insurer accepts. There is no need for further valuations.

Reinstatement value is best for the building's structure. For household contents, agreed value is ideal, because the insurer agrees upon the value of items beforehand. There is no room for dispute.

There are also several extensions that are must-buys.

- **The earthquake-damage extension** is the most obvious, because it can be excluded. It would be ironic if the incident that caused most people to buy home insurance, is excluded in the first place. Increasingly, earthquake risk is being automatically built into the insurance.
- **An escalation extension** is also useful, particularly when you buy a cost-effective, long-term cover. In multi-year insurances, inflation results in the sum assured becoming less than the replacement cost of the home. This exposes you to under-insurance. The escalation extension addresses this by automatically increasing the value of items by 10 to 25 per cent each year.
- **The omission-to-insure extension** is another useful one. This covers alterations and additions, within limits, to your home during the year without the need to inform insurers mid-term. Also covered in omission-to-insure are contents that may not have been listed out in the proposal form but are damaged.

Finally, warranties are commitments you make which if violated result in your claim being rejected.

A standard warranty is to inform the insurer if you leave the house unoccupied for over thirty days. This impacts people with second homes most. Some of my friends have a mountain-home that they visit a few times each year. In standard home insurance no claim will be paid to them unless they have informed the insurer that the house is largely unoccupied. If you have a basement then this needs to be documented. That is because basements are prone to flooding and riskier.

Another implicit condition is that of insurable interest. You cannot insure the structure of a rented home—the property owner must do that. An insurer will not question these fundamentals when you buy the insurance, but these will come to the forefront when you make a claim.

Many unresolved areas remain. Consider an apartment in a multi-storey building that is damaged by a pipe-burst. A neighbour's wall needs to be broken up for repairs but the neighbour refuses to cooperate. Home insurance will not pay for damages because repair has not been carried out. Or consider the insurance of household contents. What if all the items have not been separately specified? What if jewellery values change with fluctuating gold prices?

Policy wordings are vague and restrictive. Consider these extracts from existing contracts:

- Riots, strikes and malicious damage are covered, excluding those by: 'total or partial cessation of work or the retardation or interruption or cessation of any process or operations or omissions of any kind'. I do not know what that means.
- Or, damage due to storms, cyclones, typhoons and inundations are covered, excluding those resulting from: 'other convulsions of nature'. This one had me scurrying to my daughter's geography book.
- Fortunately, the contracts reassure us that loss due to 'missile testing operations' and 'bush fires' are covered. Sadly, damage due to 'fungi' and 'bacteria' are excluded.

A few insurers have begun to develop the market with new products. For example, agreed value as a concept can now include land cost and allow homeowners to abandon unrepairable property or under-insurance in certain cases can be corrected by paying premium retrospectively.

According to Swiss Re, a reinsurer, the floods in Jammu & Kashmir in 2014 destroyed 2 lakh houses. The loss from housing was USD 4.4 billion and less than 5 per cent of this was insured. The same year average insured losses in North America were over 60 per cent of total loss. Clearly, we have a long way to go and the obvious question is what holds back much wider purchase of property insurance?

Dealing with Sky-Falls

General insurance, in India, is a poor cousin to life insurance. That is because life insurance impacts people directly whereas general insurance, consisting of products like fire, liability, engineering and marine insurance is usually bought by companies. It typically gets relegated to an unimportant compliance under the ambiguous moniker of risk management. This explains why general insurance penetration in India is just 0.94 per cent of the nation's gross domestic product (GDP) compared to the world average of 3.88 per cent.[41]

General insurance deserves more attention, because the cost of getting it wrong is high. It impacts the economic well-being of companies severely and, by extension, you as much as life insurance. I am using a few well-recognized catastrophes to illustrate the kinds of issues in general insurance.

- **In 2004, a shipper claimed damages for four barges destroyed in the tsunami that hit our east coast:** This claim was rejected on the grounds that the tsunami was caused by an earthquake, which was excluded in the insurance. The decision was contested and the Madras High Court finally concluded that the claim was payable. It took twelve years for this decision to be taken by the courts. I discussed this case with a London-based marine insurance expert, who said that insurance clauses in the US and Europe were routinely amended to include earthquakes and that such a claim rejection would generally have not taken place there.

- **The Museum of Natural History in Delhi**: Established in 1978, it burned down on 26 April 2016. Most exhibits were destroyed. I now wish I had spent more time in the museum rather than the chaat stalls at the nearby Bengali Market. Did insurance cover the costs of restoring the museum or did the burden fall on the taxpayer?

This is not public information but the museum would have had to grapple with some issues. The first would have been to determine the value of the destroyed artifacts. Standard fire insurance values contents at book value, depreciated over time. That would be meaningless in the museum's case, because the items were acquired many years ago and, in several instances, a purchase price would not have been available. This issue can be resolved if the value of contents is set on an agreed-value basis that captures the replacement cost of items. I hope that was done.

Standard fire contracts restrict the sum assured of curios or works of art to lesser amounts. That restriction should also have been removed in the museum's insurance. Finally, there is the matter of under-insurance. If the insurer determines that the museum had a sum assured less than the actual value of the goods then any claim payment is likely to be proportionately reduced. The implication of any of these seemingly small decisions will run into millions of dollars.

- **The forest fires in Uttarakhand:** The fires raged for over eighty days in 2016. Several thousand acres of land burned down. However, forest-fire damage is an explicit exclusion in our fire insurances. Most likely the ecological and property damage in the fire would have run into billions of dollars, of which a small amount would have been insured and an even smaller amount placed properly, even when the forest-fire exclusion is removed.

  Contrast this with the forest fire that raged in Alberta, Canada about the same time. The insurance cost exceeded USD 7.5 billion and several agencies explicitly stated that forest fires were standard covers in the insurances. In many cases the cost of relocation would also have been covered.

- **31 March 2016—Collapse of the Vivekananda flyover in Kolkata:** This collapse killed over twenty-five people and injured eighty. The papers reported that the builders termed this an 'accident' and 'act of God' with alacrity. Why? Perhaps because the construction firm would have bought a 'contractor all-risk insurance' where damages due to accidents and acts of God are covered, but design defects or use of substandard materials are excluded.

  There would have been long claims discussion between the insurers and the insured on the cause of the collapse. But it is the families of those who died that will suffer most, as their claims will take years to settle. This is another example of how thinking through before buying the insurance can make a material difference.

The issue of poorly placed insurances and litigation is not unique to India. In fact there is more room for disputes overseas, because policy wordings can be changed by insurers. In India, contracts on products such as fire insurance are standardized across insurers. The main advantage that markets like the United Kingdom (UK), the US, Australia and South Africa have, is that their dispute and grievance handling is swift. Experts, knowledgeable about insurance matters, adjudicate cases.

General insurance is an area where we should welcome international expertise. Exposure and understanding in many other markets is more advanced. There is also a need to develop alternate grievance handling for general insurance claims. Currently, the Insurance Ombudsman is not allowed to handle large claims over ₹30 lakh and regular courts are the only option for that.[42] We should actively consider separate institutions to deal with larger insurance claims. Better policy wordings will also help. If you pick up any general insurance contract it is filled with cryptic phrases such as 'basement warranty', 'wait and watch warranty', 'insured versus insured', and so on. For a large number of buyers this is gibberish that becomes clear only when a claim is made.

Predicting catastrophes is hard and controlling them harder still. The step you must take to reduce your stress is to buy a well-designed home insurance.

5
Motor

～≈～

MOTOR INSURANCE IS one of the few insurances that most of you are familiar with, and have bought. First, because it is mandatory (although not everyone complies) and second, because road accidents are just so common. In fact because the frequency of claims is high, it is all the more important to know how to buy this insurance and claim successfully. Consider these situations:

- A dear uncle's car was stolen. The claim was denied because he could not furnish the original car key, which the insurer interpreted as negligence. The cost of the car was ₹4 lakh. My uncle, a retired naval officer, was, however, persistent. He approached the Insurance Ombudsman where he made an eloquent speech on how he had fought many wars for the

country but had finally been defeated by our own insurers!
The patriotic Ombudsman ordered the claim to be paid.

- During one of the heavy rains in Mumbai, a friend's car stalled on a flooded road and the engine seized. His claim was denied because of perceived negligence. He restarted the car despite it being flooded which caused the engine to seize. This cost him ₹1.5 lakh.

- A colleague met with a road accident where the car body repair cost ₹30,000. This claim was denied because my colleague's driver had not renewed his licence.

- A journalist who writes about personal finance, called me when buying her new car. She had been told by the dealer that it was mandatory for her to buy insurance from them. However, the fact is that the law specifically prohibits bundling of insurance with a new vehicle purchase. Also, the insurance was about ₹12,000 cheaper when bought from elsewhere. Her journalistic instincts saved her a tidy sum.

- A young man driving a car accidently knocked down a scooter. A huge crowd gathered and insisted that the young man compensate the scooter driver immediately, with a pay-out of at least ₹5000. My advice to the young man was not to make any settlement at all, because motor insurance works on a no-fault basis which means that the scooter owner's insurance would pay for the damage.

- A senior executive bought a spanking new BMW. A few days later the car's tyre burst. Replacing it was expensive, about ₹1 lakh. Unfortunately, the motor insurance did not cover tyre-bursts and the executive had to pay for it himself.

This section explains how to buy motor insurance both for a new car and when renewing, and importantly how to make sure your claims get paid.

What Matters in Motor Insurance?

Motor insurance is mandated by Indian law, which is why most people buy these insurances. Ideally, they should be bought to safeguard the vehicle against unforeseen damages and you should evaluate it just as you would any other insurance. Recently a friend bought a new car. He checked the car's features, took the car for a test drive and, satisfied with his choice, booked the vehicle. At the dealership my friend was filling out the necessary forms when the insurance proposal caught his eye. He asked me about the insurance and I suggested a few questions for the dealer. However, when he enquired about the policy details, the salesperson gave a blank look and said that the policy which was being offered was quite good. Unconvinced, he asked to see the insurance contract and, after some hesitation, was shown the policy that the dealership was offering. There was room for much improvement.

The practice of ignoring coverage details in a motor insurance policy is common. Most buy the motor insurance policy that the vehicle dealer offers without any research or negotiation. This is a mistake. It is often possible to get lower cost insurances and with better covers than what is available at a dealer. When you buy a motor insurance, there are certain aspects which should be considered:

- **Understand the specific risks covered under the policy:** Motor insurance plans come in two variants—third-party and comprehensive. Third-party plans cover the mandatory third-party liability which you face if you cause physical harm to any individual or damage someone's property. They do not cover the damages suffered by your own vehicle. Comprehensive plans, on the other hand, cover third-party liabilities and also the damages which are suffered by your vehicle in an accident.

- **Choose comprehensive plans:** These provide a wider coverage but the premiums are also high compared to third-party plans. If you are buying a new car or your car is not more than five years old, comprehensive plans are ideal because repair costs can be high. If, on the other hand, your vehicle is quite old or you do not use it very frequently, you can make do with third-party plans.
- **Look out for add-on covers:** Motor insurance policies offer diverse types of add-on coverage options at additional premiums. These add-ons increase the scope of coverage and can prove useful. Add-ons like roadside assistance (although many insurers have now made this a part of the base product), and zero depreciation should be chosen with a comprehensive cover. Roadside assistance provides you round-the-clock assistance if your vehicle breaks down.

  In case of zero depreciation cover, the depreciation of your vehicle's parts is ignored when a claim is made. The insurance company pays the full cost of the parts, which are repaired or replaced, without deductions. Thus, a zero-depreciation cover increases the claim pay-out. However, other add-ons should be selected only if required. For instance, the engine protect add-on is suitable if you live in an area with a problem of waterlogging or heavy rains.
- **After the coverage is secured, look out for premium discounts:** Comprehensive motor insurance policies offer several types of premium-related discounts. For instance, you can get a discount for installing safety devices, for being a member of automobile associations, for choosing a voluntary deductible and for any accumulated no-claim bonus.

  A no-claim bonus is allowed when you do not make a claim in your policy. The bonus allows a discount in the renewal premium when the policy is renewed. Moreover, you can also transfer your no-claim bonus to another policy when you sell your vehicle. Look out for these discounts to reduce your premium outgo.

So, when buying motor insurance, you should do complete research about it. You can reach out to insurance intermediaries who would do the groundwork and help recommend the best policy for your vehicle. Just make sure that when you buy the policy the vehicle details entered in the plan are correct and that the policy offers the right Insurance Declared Value (IDV).

For my friend, the value of buying the right insurance came through many months later when his car had an accident. Fortunately, the insurance company offered cashless claim settlement and the process was handled effectively with the network garage depositing the repaired car home.

Following these steps is relatively easy when you renew your insurance. You can take the time to do your research and seek options. However, this is difficult when buying a new car because your attention is on the car and not the insurance, the salespersons bundle the insurance into their proposition which makes it difficult to understand, and you are under pressure to furnish an insurance certificate to take the delivery of your car. Should you make the effort to think through the insurance then, for a new car? Yes, read on to know why.

Caveat Emptor — 'Let the buyer beware' — A Good Principle When Buying Motor Insurance from a Car Dealer

Over the past few years there have been several instances where friends buying new cars have called to check on the motor insurance they were offered at the dealer. Although, an alternate insurance may have been more economical, my friends went ahead with the dealer's offer because they felt it was better or safer in some way. That is not necessarily true.

Motor insurance, with an industry premium of about ₹65,000 crore, is the largest selling product in general insurance. It includes purchases of motor insurance when you buy a new vehicle and also when you renew insurance. The sales process for new and renewal insurance is different, but the focus over the past few years has been on new sales. This purchase takes place when you buy a new car and is, most often, bought from the car dealer itself. The sale is even more important now because recent regulations require a three-year, third-party insurance to be sold at the point of sale, rather than the erstwhile one-year product. New business insurance sales involve the automobile manufacturer (i.e., the original equipment manufacturer or OEM), dealers, intermediaries, insurers and you. This sequence also often reflects the priorities in the sales process.

New motor insurance purchase is not something most think about seriously. Why should you, when the insurance cost in proportion to the vehicle is so small. A car costing ₹10 lakh will have an insurance premium of about ₹35,000, just 3.5 per cent. And, the dealer convinces us that their insurance is best.

Much regulatory effort has gone into ensuring that buyers get a fair deal. In August 2017, the regulator issued the Motor Insurance Service Provider (MISP) regulations that clearly specified do's and don'ts for dealers and intermediaries. Two-and-a-half years later the regulator had taken several large insurance distributors to task and collectively fined them over ₹10 crore. What are the issues at stake? And how best should you buy insurance for your new car?

- **First, you are not obliged to buy motor insurance from the dealer that sells you the new car.** In fact buying elsewhere can save you money. Determining the insurance cost at a dealer can be difficult because the premium is sometimes bundled into the overall purchase cost. This is illegal. The insurance premium has to be separately stated. You should look at this and check terms outside the dealer network before buying. If you put in the effort, a savings of ₹5,000–10,0000 is possible in a ₹10 lakh-car and the amount can be much larger in more expensive vehicles.

- **Second, your dealer or motor insurance service provider (MISP) broker must offer you products from all insurers and not just a select panel.** The rationale is that panels can be selected based on the intermediary's best interest rather than that of the vehicle buyers. The regulator has come down heavily on this through hefty fines and reiterated its stand that all insurers should be allowed to compete in the dealer network.

- **Third, you cannot be induced or coerced into buying insurance from the dealer.** Insurance is a large part of a dealer's profit which is why there is considerable sales pressure. Positive inducement can take various forms, including the promise of cashless claim settlement only for insurance bought from the dealer, or a lower vehicle price, or complementary add-ons. Negative coercion can be by way of a dealer saying that buying insurance elsewhere will delay your vehicle delivery, or that claims will not be passed, or that cashless claims services will not be provided. These assertions are incorrect because most insurers will issue your new vehicle insurance, without a registration number, soon after getting a proforma invoice. Similarly, insurers do not differentiate their claim process by channel. The regulator has come down on these sales practices by levying fines in cases where dealers were incentivized by OEMs to sell insurance.

These regulatory orders are a reminder of what buyers should expect from motor insurance. Specifically, they can buy insurance from wherever they want. The MISPs must share terms from all insurers, insurance premiums must be clearly demarcated from the overall cost, and the product or claim settlement process cannot differ based on where you bought the insurance from.

The real test of your motor insurance comes when you make a claim. And claims are relatively frequent. How can you ensure that your claim is settled?

How to Ensure that Your Motor Claims are Always Paid

The most frequent insurance claims in India relate to motor accidents. Over 10,000 motor insurance claims are filed every day; in larger cities there are over 1,000 claims a day. The good news, if you can think of it like that, is that a high proportion of claims (over 95 per cent for many insurers) get paid.

The bad news is that many vehicles are not insured, people hesitate to file claims because they are unsure of the process, and claims are rejected primarily because of our own administrative lapses.

Many more vehicles would be insured if vehicle owners realized that, in accidents, they are exposed to an unlimited liability. The Motor Accident Claims Tribunal determines the compensation to accident victims or their kin. Awards are increasing in frequency and payments of over ₹50 lakh are becoming common. Without third-party insurance which, incidentally, is mandatory, you will need to pay this yourself. Over a thousand third-party claims are filed every day so this is not a risk to be ignored. Apart from third-party liability, motor insurance can also cover the cost of damage to your own vehicle. This cover called 'Own Damage' is not mandatory but worth buying because of rising repair costs.

The claim process should not intimidate you because it is simple and efficient. Take a picture of the accident, if possible. This establishes how the damage was caused. Inform the insurer on their customer service number. Have the car towed to the nearest workshop. Use your insurer's tow service if they have one. It is okay if you inform the insurer only after your vehicle reaches the workshop. These repair workshops take complete ownership of claims, from having the vehicle inspected to managing paperwork and follow-up. Increasingly, workshops are starting to offer cashless repairs where the insurer pays the workshop directly.

Most claims are rejected for five reasons that are well within our control:

- **First, the driver does not have a valid licence.** It may have expired or be for a different vehicle category or be fake.
- **Second, a personal vehicle was used as a taxi.** This issue is gaining focus across the world as car-pooling becomes commonplace.
- **Third, the insurance and vehicle are owned by different people.** This means, from an insurance perspective, the policyholder has no insurable interest in the car. It is a common issue when vehicles are resold. Sometimes the vehicle is transferred but the insurance is not or vice versa.
- **Fourth, car owners install LPG but do not register** that with the Regional Transport Office (RTO) or the insurer.

- **Fifth, owners are negligent.** They start the engine in a water-logged car (unsafe because the engine can seize) or leave the car unattended.

If these five issues are addressed, it is fairly certain that your motor claim will be paid.

A frequent complaint is that the final settled amount is less than the claim. The disagreements are mostly about vehicles that are severely damaged. The vehicle owner prefers to write-off the vehicle as a total loss, whereas the insurer will try to repair because that is cheaper. This issue has to be resolved through discussion and by depending upon the external survey reports. Another common reason for lower settlement amount is that the vehicle owner tries to get damages that have not been caused by the accident repaired. Insurers are easily able to identify such misuse.

There are some motor insurance myths that I should dispel. In an accident there is no need to establish the other driver's fault because each vehicle's insurance pays for its own damage. So, do not argue with the other driver. That just brings you unnecessary stress, plus you both block the road for everybody else. If you were at fault, that does not mean you have to pay for the other vehicle's repairs. Their insurance will pay for their repairs. All motor insurances have standard policy wordings (this is one insurance category where you do not need to read the legalese of each contract).

As mentioned earlier, the insurance you buy for new cars from dealers is prohibitively expensive. You could save thousands of rupees by buying that separately. Insurers also offer extensions and add-ons that are useful, particularly for more expensive cars. The most relevant extensions are for zero depreciation, engine seizure, and tyre repair. The zero-depreciation cover effectively allows you to get full value for damages, because no deductions are made for depreciation. Engine seizure cover is useful in areas prone to rain and waterlogging. Tyre repair is important for luxury cars, since their tyres cost a small fortune.

Finally, on a separate note, the insurer's public disclosures report over 10,000 claims every day. The Ministry of Road Transport publishes a widely cited report on road accidents according to which there are fewer than 1,500 road accidents a day. The official data gives nearly ten times lower numbers than the accident information from insurers. This should re-emphasize the point that the probability of a motor accident is relatively high and you need to understand this insurance well.

6

Travel

FALLING ILL OVERSEAS is traumatic. You are in a new country, do not know the medical system, have few known persons to reach out to, and the costs seem so much higher. Most illnesses overseas are low intensity, like a fever or a stomach upset. But occasionally, there will be something serious. That is when having the right travel insurance is invaluable. There are several considerations to be taken into account when buying travel insurance. Take the following cases:

- A few years ago my son fell ill when we were in Malaysia. The biggest challenge was to find a good doctor late at night. We did not know whom to turn to. All we could get was a paramedic who prescribed a large cocktail of drugs. My son recovered but it was stressful. The treatment cost was about ₹10,000.

- A college batchmate's son had to undergo an RT-PCR test in the UK before returning to India. The results were negative but the test itself cost about ₹31,000. We filed a claim but it was rejected on the grounds that the child was not unwell when he took the test.

- A colleague was returning from the US and her flight was held up for over a day in Dubai. The airline took care of her stay and food, but she had to make changes in her further travels that cost her about ₹15,000. This was paid by her travel insurer.

- A friend's son got into an Ivy League college for his undergraduate programme. It was expensive and the annual student insurance itself cost about ₹2.5 lakh. We found several alternate options in India that cost half as much but finally my friend decided to go with the college's identified insurance provider because she did not want to risk anything going wrong in the admission process.

- An aunt suffering from cancer wanted to visit her son in the UK. She struggled to buy travel insurance because of her age (over seventy) and her pre-existing cancer. After some research she was able to find an insurer willing to issue her a low-value cover (USD 50,000) but with a clear exclusion for pre-existing conditions. She did have severe cancer-related complications overseas and ended up spending over ₹10 lakh as out-of-pocket expenses.

- A rather haphazard friend left the country without buying health insurance. He called in a tizzy from the US asking to buy one. Unfortunately, insurers require you to be in India when you buy this insurance and we had to get my friend a special approval to buy the insurance.

These stories go to show that even something as basic as travel insurance has to be thought through. In this section you will read about the most common issues that come up and how you should address them. You'll also, learn about how to buy insurance for yourself and your child when they are studying overseas.

The Most Common FAQs on Travel Insurance Answered

With the exception of a pandemic-hit 2020, September to January is a busy period for international travel. Students join their overseas colleges, often accompanied by parents, grandparents visit their children in the winter break, and the well-heeled set out on vacation. Most international travellers buy overseas travel insurance because the cost of medical treatment abroad is prohibitive. Cardiac surgery in the US will cost about USD 100,000, for example. The Schengen countries insist on insurance as a pre-condition for their visa.[xi]

Over the years, I have received many claim intimations from international travellers. Unfortunately, many of those claims had to be rejected for the right reasons. This got me thinking that most of you do not fully understand your travel insurance. These are the questions I get asked most often.

- **Will I be insured for an existing health condition?** Most insurers do not cover hospitalization related to existing

---

xi   The Schengen Area is a group of twenty-six European countries that allow unrestricted movement of people and goods within the member countries. Each of these countries issues a Schengen visa for international visitors that allows such visitors to travel anywhere within the Schengen. (https://www.schengenvisainfo.com/)

health issues. For example, if you suffer from hypertension, cardiac claims are unlikely to be paid. A few insurers now provide limited cover for emergency treatment, even if related to existing conditions. The sum assured is restricted to about USD 10,000 in such cases. However, you must declare the existing ailment when you buy the insurance. Non-disclosure is the single biggest reason for rejecting claims. Claims will be rejected even if they are not related to the undisclosed disease.

- **If I fall ill will the payment be cashless?** If hospitalized, the process can be cashless which means that the hospital will be paid directly by the insurer. Inform your insurer as soon as you can, so that they can initiate the process. Insurers have international assistance partners who manage these claims. If there is a doubt about the claim's acceptability, for example a pre-existing condition that was not disclosed, the insurer will advise you to opt for reimbursement, i.e., you pay the bill and claim later. Outpatient claims are also covered by travel insurance and are mostly reimbursed after adjusting for a deductible of about USD 100.

- **Can a senior citizen buy overseas travel insurance?** Seniors make up a considerable proportion of overseas travellers but have the hardest time buying travel insurance. Until the age of seventy, travel insurance can be easily bought. Between seventy and eighty the number of options shrink, but it is still possible to buy. After that, most insurers will turn you down. Some insurers can sell even after eighty, but need internal underwriting approvals and will have you undergo medical tests.

  As you grow older insurers reduce the maximum sum assured that you can buy. For most countries, with the notable exception of the US, the reduced sum assured is sufficient. If a senior finds it difficult to buy insurance locally (in India), they also have the option of purchasing it in the country they visit. That is relatively expensive though.

- **Is it better to buy travel insurance in India or overseas?** Travel insurance bought in India is cheaper, but is just as effective as buying travel insurance abroad. If a fifty-year-old travelling to the US for a fortnight buys insurance in India, she will pay about ₹3,500 for a cover of USD 0.5 million. If bought overseas, it will cost twice as much.

  It is also easier to follow up later with insurers located nearby, than with those in another country. There are, however, some serious pre-existing conditions—such as cancer, cardiac ailments, strokes, and organ failure—that are not easily insurable in India and overseas insurance can be used in these cases.

- **Can I buy insurance after leaving the country?** The insurance must be bought while in India. This prevents people from buying insurance when they know they have to visit a hospital. Insurers will make an exception if you have a credible reason but it will take considerable follow-up.

- **Can I get paid if my flight is delayed or cancelled?** Insurers pay these claims if delays are caused by specific, pre-identified reasons. These could range from acts of God such as earthquakes, floods and inclement weather to fires, strikes and equipment failure. Your insurer will not pay in case of delays or cancellations caused by other reasons. Most insurers did not pay claims for flight cancellations due to the pandemic, because this was not a covered peril.

- **What if my baggage is lost or delayed?** If your entire baggage is lost and untraceable, you will be paid a specified amount. This will not cover jewellery. If just a few items from your bag are missing, those will not be paid for. In cases of delay, you will be reimbursed the cost of personal effects to manage until your bag arrives.

- **Will the cost of a COVID-19 test be covered?** If you took the test because you had symptoms and went to a doctor who gave you a written prescription to take the test, then the insurer should pay you the cost of the test. The claim amount over the deductible (typically USD 100), will be paid. The test can be expensive abroad. For example, the test in the UK can cost over £300. However, if you have undergone the test as a travel-related requirement and are asymptomatic, then the insurer may reject your claim.

So, you absolutely must buy travel insurance when going overseas. Its main benefit is if you suffer an accident or medical emergency. The insurance is less useful for routine health issues or travel-related inconveniences. Most of your trips will be short term, from a few days to perhaps a few months. However, students studying overseas throughout the year are also required by their colleges to buy insurance and this can be expensive.

Is there a cost-effective way to get student travel insurance? Counterintuitively, should you insure yourself when your child goes overseas?

Who Should Be Insured When Your Child Studies Abroad, and How?

When my daughter applied to go to college, her online test centre in Delhi's Karol Bagh colony was a veritable fire hazard. Five-hundred children, including my daughter, were cramped inside a small building with a single narrow entrance, no emergency exits, heavy electrical wiring and no water bottles, bags, food or phones allowed. I thought about taking my daughter out but then, not wanting to be classified as overprotective, stood beside hundreds of other parents for a long time in the sweltering heat.

Can't the authorities see the obvious, or do we need fires to break out in Karol Bagh hotels, cinema halls or hospitals before taking action? Buying fire insurance is not the solution to these issues but preventing an imminent fire is.[43] Eventually my daughter, like many others at this test centre, did get to go to the college of her choice.

There are some insurance decisions that you must take before the kids leave:

- **Buy your child an independent domestic health insurance:** Most children will have been a part of their parent's family-floater health insurance. These plans cover dependent children till they are somewhere between eighteen and twenty-five years old. After that they are excluded from the parent plan. You should then pro-actively transition to an independent insurance for your child.

- **The sum assured should you buy for an 18-year-old:** A ₹10 lakh health cover will cost between ₹5,000–10,000 a year. Pay twice that and you get a cover of ₹50 lakh for your child. Insurers will give them a stand-alone health insurance, without medical tests or additional declarations. This will also reduce the cost of the parent's family-floater insurance, because one less family member is covered.

- **Studying overseas is terribly expensive:** An undergraduate degree in the US or UK costs between ₹1.5–3 crore. Asian and European colleges cost less but are still expensive. To add to that, the student's international insurance is a major cost when studying overseas.

- **Universities are specific about the insurance cover you must have:** Sometimes there is no option but to buy what the college demands.

  In the UK: Visa authorities add an International Health Surcharge to allow students to access the National Health Scheme (NHS) and many parents also buy an additional private cover because accessing non-emergency specialist care through the NHS can take much longer than what we are used to here.

  In Australia: It is mandatory to buy insurance from approved Australian insurers.

  If you are allowed to buy student insurance in India, the cost-saving can be significant. For example, in the US, an insurance plan that costs over ₹3 lakh a year will cost under ₹1 lakh here. However, this purchase needs to be carefully researched, because you do not want to buy something that is not accepted by the college or visa authorities.

  Ideally, ask the university to certify that the insurance you are buying in India is okay with them. If there is an issue, the student's insurance will be fully refunded before travel commences.

  Finally, given the prohibitive cost of overseas education, you must insure yourself against death while your child studies. You are likely to be between forty-five to fifty-five years old if your child is entering college and, if healthy, accident is the most probable cause of death. This can be specifically covered by personal accident insurance with a high sum assured of ₹1–2 crore.

  Until recently, these high-value insurances were not available but are now more common. However, they may not be listed on the insurer's website so you'll need to reach out to an adviser or the company to buy these. A sum assured of ₹2 crore, will cost about ₹25,000 per year.

These accident insurances can be bought even if you suffer from chronic conditions such as diabetes or hypertension and can be discontinued once your child completes their education.

My daughter is now studying law at the National Law University, Jodhpur. They have an MBA in insurance and I have suggested that once this book is published, I could visit her campus and give some guest lectures. By being close to her I can sort out these possible health and hazards. For some inexplicable reason my daughter does not not share my enthusiasm and is busy dissuading me.

PART 2

Processes

7

Buying and Claiming

THE PREVIOUS SECTION described insurance products and the risks they address. However, in insurance, it is not just the product that is important but also the buying and claiming process. The principles discussed here cut across insurance products. Following a disciplined process prevents surprises. Consider these examples:

- One of my cousins has a health insurance with a sum assured of ₹5 lakh. This insurance has been running for several years and all waiting periods are over. Recently, his wife was diagnosed with breast cancer and the treatment costs so far have been about ₹20 lakh. The out-of-pocket cost is ₹15 lakh and this has been difficult to put together.
- A senior executive bought an expensive, gold-plated insurance from a health insurer because he felt that it was a good brand.

This insurance cost about ₹1.5 lakh. However, several of his claims were initially rejected and required considerable follow-up to be approved. He was left wondering whether he had overspent and should have instead bought cheaper insurances from providers with better settlement rates.

- A colleague bought a motor insurance because it was about ₹5,000 cheaper than all the other options that he had. However, when he had an accident and filed a claim, he was rather shocked to see that only ₹60,000 of his ₹90,000 bill was paid, because this low-cost insurance deducted depreciation and did not cover tyres. He would have been better off paying the additional ₹5,000 while buying the insurance.

- A batchmate travelling overseas posted on a social-media-group of friends asking which travel insurance to buy. There were five suggestions based on everybody's first-hand experience and he selected one. During his travel, my friend, who was diabetic, had to visit an emergency room because of a sudden increase in his sugar level. The bill was USD 2,400 and the insurer turned it down because issues related to pre-existing conditions were excluded. Had my friend depended less on social media perspectives and more on research and informed opinion, he would have picked an insurance that covered emergency care even for pre-existing conditions.

- A business colleague bought a life insurance where the agent told him that he could earn as much as 25 per cent per annum based on the insurer's track record. His actual returns were 10 per cent over a five year period. Not bad, but well below his expectation. Had he read the formal illustration that came with the policy copy he would have seen that the insurer clearly specified a range of 4 to 8 per cent returns. From the insurer's perspective they had outperformed, yet my colleague felt let down.

- A client kept ignoring the repeated messages to renew her insurance. These messages came from the insurer and an intermediary over emails, the phone and via SMS. Six months after the life insurance had lapsed the client decided to renew her insurance. To her surprise the insurer refused to renew it because she had developed hypertension over the past year. The client had no choice but to buy a new insurance that cost her ₹27,000 more than her initial policy of ₹50,000.

Following processes painstakingly can be boring. But in insurance it helps in getting you a product that really works to make you financially secure. This section outlines the steps you must meticulously take to buy any insurance.

The First Step in Buying Insurance

Your life, health and home have a value that must reflect in the amount of insurance you buy. Determining this amount, though, can be an art.

A substantial number of deaths lower life's perceived value. Coronavirus deaths have become a statistic within a curve that we want flattened. In the US, *The New York Times* tried to prevent reducing people to numbers by dedicating a front page to the first 100,000 deaths and listing their memories gathered from obituaries. In the military skirmishes on our borders, the value of life sometimes gets reduced to a counting of which side has more casualties.

I have, over the years, answered how much life insurance to buy in diverse ways. The most rational is to project future expenses and revenue, if you die prematurely. Life insurance should fill the gap. Few follow this approach because it is elaborate and unemotional. I have sometimes suggested a thumb rule to buy a sum assured in insurance that is ten times one's annual income. This is easier to understand because it is built on the concept that, should you die prematurely, the sum assured by the insurance will cover ten years of income. This would allow the family time to find its financial feet. The challenge in this approach is that the cost of buying enough insurance to provide such a large sum assured is high, and most are not willing to buy that much insurance. I encourage people to buy what they can and begin with one insurance instead of being paralysed into inaction.

The most effective purchases, however, are those where the insurance amount is linked to a specific objective. This is an emotional appeal but with facts. Aspirations that buyers state when buying insurance, include: 'I would like my daughter to study in Oxford (or some other good college, for that matter)'; 'I would like to leave a gift for my husband'; or 'I would like my family to own a house'. These aspirations have a quantifiable value and I jump at the opportunity to specify that amount as the sum assured in a term-life insurance. The Oxford education costs over a crore of rupees; a meaningful gift, a crore or two; and a home in an upscale metropolis will cost between ₹4–10 crore.

The aspiration, cited often, that makes me uncomfortable is marriage expenses for a daughter, often with the benefit timed to the child turning twenty-one. I wish the industry would not market this. When I was working at Unilever, over two decades ago, the possibility of a certain brand of cream dropping references to fairness, whiteness or light skin, was unthinkable. But this has now happened. Insurers can take a cue and encourage a broader perspective.

Another shift is in health insurance's sum assured. Historically, the estimates we used were up to ₹10 lakh for cardiac care in a good, city hospital and ₹10–15 lakh for cancer treatment. So, a sum assured of ₹10–20 lakh was safe territory. COVID-19 has changed the equation. Treatment costs have crossed ₹10 lakh in many private hospitals, and even non-COVID-19 disease treatment costs have increased substantially.

Hospital capacity is under pressure; hygiene and treatment protocols are escalating costs. In these conditions, a sum assured of ₹20–30 lakh rather than ₹10–20 lakh is needed in the metropolitan cities, particularly for families. I prefer insurances that are wider in their scope of cover. Specific disease insurances are useful after you have the basic insurances in place. First, increase your mediclaim sum assured to the right level then buy more specialized insurances.

Finally, your home. This is the most significant asset you own and the sum assured is particularly important. Home insurances typically pay for repair costs after the repair is done. In such cases, the sum assured should be equal to the construction cost of a new house. However, in the case of high-rises, the damage in another apartment may make your apartment unliveable; or disputes between the builder, homeowners and service providers may delay reinstatement. In such situations, you should be able to buy a new home and the sum assured should cover that cost. This means you need to have a home insurance that pays not just for repairs, but also for the land cost inherent in an apartment's price.

The decision on the sum assured is not a once-done-and-finished decision. Every so often, but certainly on renewal, you should go through what you have see bought and whether the coverages need to be increased.

Once you know the sum assured you need, the next step is to select an insurer. It is not easy because there are over fifty insurers focused on various products. How then does one make the choice?

The Science behind Choosing an Insurer

I am often asked who the 'best' insurers are. I try to dodge that question because the answer requires a detailed analysis of what one is looking for. When Alice, in Lewis Carroll's *Alice in Wonderland*, asks which way she should go, the Cheshire cat wisely replies, 'That depends a great deal on where you want to get to'. Insurer selection, however, would have flummoxed the Cheshire cat because in insurance, even if you know where you want to get to, it is hard to get the data that helps you find your way.

Let us say that you want an insurer who has the best claims record. For that you must know the claim settlement rates by product, claim payment times, claim complaints, extent of litigation, who wins the legal cases and how often the insurer pays interest on late claim payment. Some of this information is available, but much of it is not or is available in aggregate form. For example, you can get overall claim settlement rates but these are not published by product. Details of litigation are not available, though I am sure an enterprising analyst could go to all the district, state, consumer and Ombudsman courts to put this together.

There are other relevant areas where no information is available, for example, in the quality of policy placement. This is an important consideration because every single insurance buyer is impacted by it. The requirement here is to measure items such as clarity of coverage, error-free policy contracts and timely endorsements—but there is no public information on this.

The Insurance Brokers Association of India, where I am a director, decided to address this lack of synthesized information by developing two documents: first, a claims handbook;[44] and second, a survey of brokers to get their assessment of various insurers. These are both extremely useful. The brokers' voice, particularly, merits attention. Brokers represent clients through a formal mandate; typically, Brokers work with several insurers and get a privileged view into insurance processes such as placement, grievance handling and claims that are required to evaluate an insurer's performance.

The IBAI survey asked all brokers ten questions. These were strung around the themes of broker orientation, handling claims and grievances, quality of policy placement and technology experience. In all, 137 insurance brokers responded and their senior executives or business owners completed the survey. We followed the Net Promoter Score (NPS) method of ranking. This system provides a net score that is the difference between promoters (those that gave a high 9 or 10 score) and detractors (those that gave a score of 7 or less). Our focus was on general and health insurers; life insurers were left out. Among the general insurers, the top quartile insurers were Tata AIG, ICICI Lombard, Bajaj Allianz, HDFC Ergo, Go Digit, New India, IFFCO Tokio, and Reliance General.[45] These insurers were the leaders based on brokers' responses to the question, 'How likely are you to recommend these insurers to your industry peers?'

Not all awards are created equal. I have been on some juries where assessment has been superficial. Readers would do well to consider only those awards seriously that have been peer-reviewed, have a quantitative foundation, do not require payment and are objective. Such awards nudge companies to improve and focus on policyholders. The awards by the IBAI fall into that category.

Once you have a subset of two or three insurers, based on informed opinion, you need to pick your product from amongst those offered by these insurers. Our tendency is to pick the cheapest product. That is a mistake.

How Important is Price?

Never judge a book by its cover and never judge an insurance just by its price. Equally important is an insurer's claims payment and complaint-handling ability. Every claim or complaint is different, so it is impossible to predict an insurer's specific response. But this is one situation where past performance is an indicator of the future.

Over the years, I have seen hundreds of claims across business lines and there are many differences in the way insurers react when faced with a claim. Several will move fast and close the matter with a quick decision. With some others, the tendency may be to find fault. A few claims require a surveyor to make an assessment. In theory the surveyor should make a completely independent recommendation of loss. In reality, there is a bias to go along with the insurer's perspective.

The ideal insurer handles many claims, decides fast, in favour of claimants and still turns out an underwriting profit. This is somewhat like being a superhero. An unattainable gold standard. However, at the very least, buyers must look into available claims information to determine where an insurer falls against this gold standard.

An insurer who handles many claims is more likely to have good processes in place. Such processes are important because claims come in large numbers with considerable diversity, and poor systems can lead to wrong decisions. Claim numbers are large and increasing. In the fiscal year 2021, insurers handled over 110,000 general insurance claims and 5,900 death claims every single day.[46] Does this mean that insurers handling fewer claims should not be selected? I would say that unless you are an informed buyer, there may be safety in numbers.

Turning claims around fast is not easy. Much work needs to be done before a decision can be taken. For example, in motor or property damage, a surveyor has to be appointed within a day or two. In health-related cases, or accidents, or death, the claim papers must be speedily assessed and a thoughtful response sent to customers. Often, the insurer may have to settle a cashless claim within an hour. This quick response is important because, when an accident or hospitalization occurs, most claimants are in distress and looking for fast solutions.

In many commercial cases, as time passes, it becomes difficult to assess the claim. For one public-sector insurer, over one-third of claims related to fire and liability took over six months to settle. For a large private sector insurer, over 20 per cent of the outstanding claims were over a year old. To be fair the delay may be because the claimant has not furnished all the information. Still, it is a warning if these numbers are too high.

Claim settlement rates indicate whether decisions favour policyholders. These are expressed in terms of number of policies and also in terms of value. I find the metric of the number of policies more relevant to buyers, because this gives a better feel of how small claims are managed. Claim settlement has many definitions and you should look at these carefully. The best definition takes positive claim decisions on a base of total decisions taken. Finally, an underwriting profit is generated when total claims and expenses are less than total premium. If an insurer continuously suffers losses, it will come under pressure to cut claims either in terms of the claim acceptance itself or in terms of the claim-value paid.

Complaining is never easy, particularly to insurers. When I think about grievance cells, I visualize the fierce looking commando at the metro station in MG Road, Gurugram. He is hidden behind a metal bunker, only machine gun and eyes visible. Handwritten on the enclosure is a sign that says, 'No enquiries here please'. Quite unwelcoming[47],yet those that must find their way will approach the commando. This is the case with grievance cells as well. An aggrieved claimant will complain no matter how difficult the process.

The performance of policyholder complaints can be determined by the number of complaints per 10,000 policies and its aging. The differences amongst insurers are large, the best being half or one-third the average. All of this information is readily available from several sources such as the IRDAI's annual reports, statistical updates, public disclosures of insurers on their websites and a handbook published by the IBAI. However, getting to the information you want requires filing through all the papers and, sometimes, calculating numbers yourself to ferret out the right metrics.

A good adviser can help you through this process but you will have to ask the tough questions and not take recommendations at face value. Your relationship with the insurance adviser is important to get the best outcomes. But what does a good relationship require?

The Need for Respect and Reasonable Expectations

Buying insurance is an intense process. You share intimate details on your health and income, subjecting yourself to scrutiny from insurers. When things go wrong in this process, the instinctive reaction is to blame the insurer or salesperson. However, you are also at fault sometimes.

I am reminded of this when, a few times every month, I take individual customer calls. These are not the cold calls that we dislike but are from people who've reached out to us for insurance. In these meetings or calls, I introduce myself as a salesperson rather than co-founder. I confess that, even though I love what I do, these discussions are not fun, often because of the aggression and unrealistic expectations of buyers.

This confrontational relationship between the salesperson and the customer leads to poor insurance outcomes. A badgered salesperson sees no long-term benefit in a relationship and just wants to get over with the sale. A harassed underwriter has no incentive to suggest solutions for getting insured. I sometimes feel that the very process of buying health insurance worsens your health, an example of the Heisenberg Effect, according to which the very act of observing something changes the thing being observed. This is your loss because a poor outcome impacts you the most. How can you be a good customer? Here are some pointers.

- **Do not talk down to the salesperson:** Do not tell a salesperson that their company is no good, or that you are going to complain to someone senior if your insurance is not issued, or show exasperation if the salesperson has difficulty following English, or yell at the salesperson when they inform you about problems with your insurance.[48]

  The salesperson may be from a socio-economic class different from yours but this does not make them incompetent at their job. In fact, it makes them stand out. I find sales applicants from middle-class and poor families or smaller towns have a drive and commitment that is unmatchable.

  The real handicap that a salesperson faces is that they cannot answer back. In our cultural context, answering back would result in them getting fired. We should remember that many of us started our careers on the front line, I certainly did. Ask them for as much information as you want, as many times, but do so courteously.

- **Give them all the facts:** Here is a typical customer conversation:

  Me: 'You said you had no health problems?'

Customer: 'I don't.'

Me: 'But your report says you have had diabetes for fifteen years?'

Customer: 'That's not a disease—you should know better.'

Replace diabetes with any disease and I have had that conversation.

Concealing information just does not work, apart from the fact that it is unethical. Insurers have strong underwriting teams that can extract information that you have concealed. Even if the insurance does get issued, your claim will not be paid because pre-existing diseases are captured in discharge summaries, internal case reports and operation-theatre records. Instead, give the insurer an accurate view of your medical history or previous claims. They want to get the insurance done and will most likely give you practical tips. Sometimes, the solution may be to buy a sum assured less than the medical threshold, or select a different benefit structure.

- **Have realistic service expectations:** Service processes and systems are poor; insurers have much to improve. Website calculators do not work (or two calculators on the same website give different premiums for a product). Questions remain unanswered (particularly those that are directed to generic email IDs). Routine information requests are made sequentially rather than in one go. Facts in the contract are wrong (I spent a month trying to get the spelling of 'bubbles' in a policy correct).[49]

    Sadly, a salesperson has little ability to influence these issues. What they can do is to help you navigate the system smoothly. Your expectations also need to be realistic. You often take months to make up your mind and put together basic documents—a proposal form, identity and address proof. However, you expect the insurer to turn around applications in days.

- **Respect the salesperson's time:** Before the pandemic, I worked thrice a week from Gurugram and the remaining time from Delhi. My meetings were grouped to minimize travel time and, like most executives, I am particular about time being used properly.

  Salespersons are unable to do this because they are often called to meet clients for relatively routine matters, for example to fill a proposal form. Customers ought to be able to do this themselves. Instead, the salesperson waits while the form is being filled. It takes a couple of meetings to get the documentation done. Appointments get rescheduled without informing salespersons. A client recently complained that he wanted a salesperson to meet and follow-up with him a few times because that is what he was used to. Salespersons quickly realize that after adjusting for travel and time costs, they earn little money.

  Today, the need for a physical meeting is decreasing. Forms and payments can be completed online. Document pick-ups are co-ordinated by couriers. Value the salesperson's time and use it for advice and perspective rather than clerical activity.

- **Finally, recognize that advice has value:** Do not play one insurer or salesperson off another, make one person do the work and then buy from someone else. In motor insurance this issue is endemic. A salesperson will share options, negotiate discounts. The client will then use the negotiated price of one salesperson to buy from another, more favoured insurer. The issue here is that the salesperson who provided the advice earned nothing. Over time this has disincentivized the system to invest in quality advice.

There are tangible advantages to being a good customer: the insurer will place the insurance properly, claims will get paid, and the salesperson will go the extra mile for you. Apart from these tangible benefits, being good is, simply put, just the right thing to do.

You need to know your insurance advisor, and her/his motivations, better. How do you go about that?

The Unsung Heroes Selling Insurance

I would not like to be an insurance agent. Research regularly reconfirms that it is one of the professions that is most looked down upon in the US, Australia, UK, most of Asia, and India. In the Gallup polls conducted in the US between 1977 and 2012, 30–45 per cent of the respondents consistently averred that insurance agents had low ethics and honesty. The US members of Congress fare worse but, unlike insurance agents, they are rich.

This stereotyping is unfortunate because it has resulted in a vicious cycle where good people shy away from insurance as a profession. Recently, I spoke with a leading insurance adviser in the Middle East. His entire family has been in this business, yet he laughed as he said that nobody graduates from college with the intention of getting into insurance. Even if good people were to sign-up, success is difficult. The combination of skills required for an agent to succeed is difficult to find.

In 2003, when the insurance sector had just opened up I took, for a lark, the psychometric test that prospective agents must take to qualify. To my surprise, I failed. I walked up to the CEO of the insurer where I worked and told him to save company money by scrapping these tests. Wise man that he was, the

CEO suggested I 'dig deeper' and dismissed me.[50] I did that and discovered the combination of character traits needed for success as an insurance agent: perseverance, empathy and extroversion.

- **Perseverance** keeps agents going when friends and family turn away; when closing a sale takes months. A leading Indian-origin agent in the US once took me for a drive in his S-Class Mercedes through Edison, New Jersey. What made him so successful? It turns out that when he went to the US twenty years ago and took an insurance licence, an uncle had looked away when he'd seen his agent-nephew approach. That incident made him determined to become so good at his work that people would seek him out for advice. I once met a seventy-year-old leading Taiwanese agent at an international sales convention. She became an insurance agent to send her grandchildren to college. Over five years, she established the most successful agency in Taiwan and attended the convention accompanied by her now college-going grandchildren. Good insurers search for people who have adeptly handled adversity in their lives. This is the best surrogate for perseverance.
- **Empathy** helps the agent relate to the buyer's, build a rapport and recommend the right products. Empathy comes when the agent's life stage is similar to the buyer. An agent with children understands the need to plan for college education; the sixty-year-old agent knows the importance of health insurance for senior citizens. This is one profession where being young is a deterrent because of the generation gap between buyer and seller.
- **Finally, extroversion**—the reason I failed the psychometric test. An agent acquires new customers by putting his hand out and introducing himself. Most of us are uncomfortable

doing that because we fear rejection. Agents take rejection in their stride, because deep down they are convinced that selling insurance is a good thing. This is so important for you to understand. The insurance agent is not looking to sell you some horrible products and then disappear. In fact, many agents themselves buy the products they sell to you.

Why then are agents hated so much and why are so many of you dissatisfied with your insurances? The reason is poorly designed products and ineffective complaint resolution. There is a huge responsibility on insurers and regulators to make sure products introduced in the market are fair. Importantly, you must have a respectable exit if you change your mind about your insurance. In 2005, after I had been in the insurance industry for some time, I bought a whole life plan. Despite being from the industry, I had not realized the high penalties that would apply if I left the insurance midway. When I surrendered the policy, I lost about 20 per cent of the premiums paid.

Recently a friend approached me with a unique problem. He had bought a pension plan that matured about a year ago. Given his financial circumstances he wanted to withdraw the accumulated funds rather than convert them into an annuity, even if it meant paying tax or a surrender penalty. The insurer refused and the funds were transferred to the insurer's general account. Now the only option for my friend was to buy an annuity that would pay him a fixed amount over the years. Had the person applied for his money a day before maturity, the full amount would have been paid, but after maturity, nothing. The insurer's decision is consistent with the contract, even though the contract itself is unfair. Blaming the agent for such issues is like shooting the messenger.

It is a myth that agents are rich with commissions. The average premium for an insurance policy is less than ₹20,000, on which commissions are about ₹4,000. Only the best agents sell two to four policies a month. This means that the earning of high performers is about ₹10,000–15,000 a month. In 2014, fewer than 7,000 agents earned over ₹75,000 a month. Hardly a king's ransom. Factor in discounts that buyers routinely ask for and the income is further depleted. Also, it takes three to five meetings to close a sale. That is why only 15 per cent of the 2 million registered life insurance agents are active in the sense that they sell an insurance policy each month.

A good agent can provide you all the information you need. Yet we turn to social media for answers. Is that a good idea?

Unfollow Social Media for Insurance

In 2019, I was at the Jama Masjid during Ramzan. The courtyard was teeming with people watching the sun set and waiting to break their fasts. As I looked out through the arches at the beautiful Red Fort, I could imagine Shah Jahan doing the same 350 years ago, except, of course, for the official notice at the entrance that said 'No TikTok videos allowed'.

Social media has cast its net wide and insurance is just about getting ensnared. Most insurers are on Facebook, Twitter and some on Instagram. Some of these sites have large following. One large insurer has over 2 million Facebook followers. For many others the followers range from 200,000 to a million. I checked TikTok, before it was banned, but no insurer seemed active there yet. Insurers engage on social media to share information and hear grievances.

Social media sites is poor source of information for insurance. The material is mostly copied from the internet. One post, obviously drawn from the US, advised me to use aniseed for a healthier life and I had to turn to Google to learn they meant *saunf*. Another post spoke about how insurance can mitigate inheritance tax. This is fine, except this tax does not exist in India. Insurers also share their advertisements and new product launches. There is a bland sameness to this information. The information is similar across social media platforms because publishing tools are used to distribute the same content across all of them.

Social media could be an excellent grievance redressal mechanism, but there is something in the medium that unhinges people. On unmoderated sites the comments come across as rants. 'Worst company ever', 'Don't buy from them', 'U r terrible' seem to be the most common. However, these comments lack substance and when I have tried to go deeper, often there is no meaningful complaint, just an attempt to extort a benefit. Genuine complaints suffer because insurers switch off from social media comments. The official responses are mostly canned replies redirecting the complainant to an email ID or customer care number.

Many insurers now prohibit unmoderated comments on their pages. You can observe this, as their posts are greeted by an army of appreciators about the 'awesome' product being launched. An issue from the regulatory standpoint is that social media complaints are not defined as a grievance for reporting. If you must use social media to complain, then Twitter is the most effective. However, the best way to get yourself heard by insurers remains the old-fashioned email.

Speaking of email, you must be cautious about phishing, a common fraud. Phishing can take several forms. You will receive an email requesting payment through electronic means or a payment link. The electronic transfer will be to an account not owned by the insurer. In fact, sometimes even if the account name looks similar to the insurer the account can be a personal one. Similarly, the payment link will redirect money to a personal account. When you transfer money in this way the insurer has no liability and you stand to lose your entire payment.

You can prevent such fraud by verifying that the email you received for payment is from the company itself. The domain should be the company's own. When you click on a payment gateway it should be one of the well-recognized payment portals and the insurer's name must be clearly specified. Insurers will also generally display your policy details for confirmation. If you are not using an electronic payment option, never hand over cash to a salesperson or write out a cheque to someone other than the insurer. The insurer's full legal name is always mentioned in the footer on their websites. Insist on a receipt from the insurer and intermediary.

Insurance also has a solution for some of these risks, a personal cyber-liability cover. These will pay for financial losses related to phishing and cost about ₹6,000 for a sum assured of ₹20 lakh. They also insure for some other online risks such as trolling and cyberbullying, but those covers are currently extremely restrictive. For example, the trolling cover will pay the cost of treatment by a mental health professional if it is established that trolling resulted in your condition.

At the Jama Masjid, after the fast was broken, I looked around to see if anybody was defying the 'No TikTok videos' notice. They were not. Instead, all the youngsters had rushed out to Qureshi where succulent kebabs won over TikTok hands down. Social media still has some catching up to do.

So let us say that you have used informed opinions and data-led research, rather than social media, to decide on an insurer and the specific product to buy. The next step is to share your personal and medical information with the insurer through a proposal form. This is an important document—how should you complete this?

The Severe Consequences of Not Reading and Filling the Proposal Form Yourself

Buying insurance requires considerable paperwork. Brochures and key-feature documents need to be read, illustrations and declarations signed, financial and know-your-customer (KYC) information submitted. The most important document, however, is the humble proposal form.

This proposal form comes in different shapes and sizes. In many cases it is paper-based and needs to be filled by hand. Sometimes, the information can be provided electronically, and, in a few cases, such as motor insurance, the proposal form may not even be required.

The form is important, obviously, because that is where you provide information that forms the basis of your insurance. But, equally valuable, is the fact that completing a proposal form requires putting pen to paper or fingers to keyboard. The act of writing forces mindfulness. The few minutes it takes to complete a proposal form is when you understand the product best, specifically the features and the claims that will get paid.

- **In filling up a proposal form you should be accurate:** That is easier said than done. The most basic information asked is your contact details. Yet, crores of claims and maturity amounts remain unpaid because insurers are unable to reach policyholders at the numbers and addresses they gave. Do ensure that the address you give is permanent, the phone number is one that you intend to keep and the email ID is personal. People change jobs more often than they expect.

- **Provide the information asked and no more:** Be to the point. There is little benefit in giving additional information. There have been situations, in health insurance for example, where the applicant opened up about feeling anxious and had their application declined. In motor insurance, there is little advantage to describing small dents if they are not asked for, particularly if the insurance is getting renewed on time. The insurer may exclude those damages or ask for an inspection, both of which are a hassle.

- **Complete the form yourself:** That allows you to control what is shared. All too often applicants sign a blank proposal form and have an adviser do the rest. That is a recipe for disaster. It is not that the adviser will deliberately misstate facts but there may be information they are unaware of or, in their wisdom, they may leave out things they consider unimportant.

- **When insurers send back a copy of the completed proposal form, read it:** This is an important check to see the basis on which the insurance is being issued. Sometimes, information may be altered by someone in the distribution chain and it is good to look out for such inconsistencies.

- **For life insurance, in particular, the nominee section in the proposal form is key:** Previously, the benefits of a life insurance policy were paid to the legal heirs with the nominee being a temporary custodian of the money. However, according to the new insurance act, if the nominees you select in the proposal form are legal heirs then the entire benefit will be paid to them in the proportion you specify.[51] This gives you much better control on directing who should benefit from your insurance.

- **Select insurers who design their proposal forms to be brief, specific and educative:** The length of proposal forms varies hugely amongst insurers. In home insurance, they range from two to six pages; in health insurance, from three to twelve. Lengthy forms have two problems. First, the formatting is poor, making them cumbersome to fill. It is often not possible to write legibly in the form. Second, you are never sure which information is mandatory and whether the fields you left out are the ones that will matter when you make a claim.

- **For home insurance, make sure you address, in the proposal form, the main reasons for claim rejection. These are:** The basement (where the loss often occurs) was not declared; commercial activity (such as an office or clinic) was not mentioned; the length of time the house would remain vacant was not listed. In a good form all these questions should be specifically asked, to reduce the possibility of a claim being rejected. Health insurance has a similar need for specificity. Specificity is required while filling in a form.

- **Look for an insurer whose catch-all questions are more specific:** For example, 'Are you currently suffering from any symptom(s) or complaint(s) that have been persisting for more than five consecutive days?' or 'Have you undergone any surgery or has a surgery been advised to you in the last ten years?' Such specific questions leave less scope for disputes and are better from your perspective. All health insurance forms have catch-all medical questions that require applicants to mention diseases they suffer from.

  Some insurers cover these broadly and ask questions that always leave applicants doubtful about what to declare. For example, 'Have you had any illness other than the ones mentioned in the questionnaire (or other than common cold)?' or 'Any additional facts which affect the insurance and should be disclosed to the insurer?'

- **Finally, a good proposal form educates you about the insurance once more:** It will tell you that in a home insurance there is a choice between reinstatement value (where cost of reconstruction is paid), or the market value (where depreciated value is paid). In a motor insurance, it will clearly specify the exclusions (such as engine seizure or tyre bursts) and the add-ons. In health insurance, it will remind you of the waiting periods for diseases.

You should take your time to fill this form. Remember, those who act in haste repent at leisure.

There is one last step before you can relax and that is to carefully read the policy docket, particularly the contract when it arrives. But what should you look for in the contract?

Trust, but Verify Your Policy Contract

Buying insurance, particularly term or health, can be an elaborate process. Forms are to be filled, KYC documents provided, medical tests conducted and payments made. So, when the insurer tells you that the insurance is done, most heave a sigh of relief, and file the insurance contract somewhere. Do not do that. There is one final step before you can switch off, and that is to read the policy kit.

The first page of the policy contract captures the most critical information about your insurance, and if it is not correct you run the risk of delays in claim payment or even claim rejection. Mistakes on this page do take place. These are mostly errors that can and should be corrected immediately.

- **In life and health insurance check six details in the final policy documents thoroughly:** Personal information, nominees, illustrations, the submitted proposal form, special endorsements and the insurance start date. This will take you all of five minutes but can save your family months of effort if a claim is made. Incorrect personal information, such as a misspelled name or wrong date of birth, will require extensive documentation to correct when a claim is filed. If you are hospitalized they will compare details on your contract with your identity documents. Mismatches result in delayed approvals. A nominee should be correctly named and the relationship with you specified.

- **Read the copy of your proposal form carefully:** This has often been a cause of disagreement because most sign a blank form and leave it to an adviser to complete. In the case of health insurance your own medical history and that of your family's must be accurate.

- **Make sure you agree with the diseases listed as pre-existing by the insurer:** A friend suffered from joint pain in one hand and the pre-existing diseases listed excluded any coverage for her orthopaedic condition. In another case, someone with an injury in one eye had all eye-related treatments excluded. These pre-existing conditions listed in the insurance policy can be corrected if you request for specificity. Diseases that you have been declared should be clearly listed in your policy. Recently a friend realized that they had a fake policy issued by the salesperson, because a declared cardiac ailment was not listed.

- **While reading the proposal form, look for inaccuracies even if they do not seem important to you:** An overstated income may be problematic, because the insurer could question the amount of insurance you have. A family history of diabetes, not listed in the proposal, may be treated as material non-disclosure.

- **Read the life insurance illustration in your contract kit:** You should have seen and signed this document before. This is the most reliable way to understand what you have bought. If you thought that you have bought a limited-pay insurance but the illustration shows payments throughout the policy, then that must be corrected. If a promised guarantee is not shown in the illustration it will not be paid.

  Particularly in life insurance, there can be many special conditions under which the insurance is bought, such as the Married Women's Protection Act (MWPA) or Keyman. The MWPA ensures that your insurance cannot be attached against any liability you may have. This is used by business owners who give personal guarantees to ringfence their insurances. If your insurance does not have such an endorsement then you cannot protect it under the MWPA. Similarly, Keyman insurance has to be marked as such, because in a Keyman the claim is paid to the company rather than the employee.

- **The date when you first bought the insurance is most important:** All waiting periods are calculated from this date onwards.

  In health insurance: this waiting period is specified. It begins from the time your insurance becomes operational and lasts for the number of years (two, four, etc.) mentioned in your insurance. During this waiting period no hospitalization or treatment— for any disease you already had before buying this insurance—will be covered by the insurance.

  In life insurance: it marks the start of the three-year period after which a claim cannot be contested by the insurer. Sometimes the start date gets reset if you make any changes in the insurance or if there is a system change at the insurer.

  Reading the first page of the contract is important in other insurances as well: In a home insurance, verify that the address is correct and your basement or terrace is listed in the insurance. These can later become reasons for claim rejection.

These checks must be done each year: In annually renewable insurances, such as health and home insurance, changes from year to year do happen and you do not want to be caught on the wrong side of this mistake.

Congratulations if you have reached so far and completed these checks. You now have good insurances that secure you from most unexpected risks. Stop thinking about your insurances, until the renewal a year later. But why is a renewal so important?

The One Payment You Should Never Ever Miss

Recently I was reviewing a life insurance claim. The policyholder had died after paying premium for several years. Unfortunately, as things turned out, the last premium was unpaid and the claim was denied. I was disappointed because the lost benefit ran into lakhs.

A familiar scene at insurance renewal time is insurers and intermediaries pursuing policyholders. However, for most insurances the worst impact of a policy lapsing is on the policyholder, not the insurer. There is a loss of cover but also a loss of many key benefits linked to renewal.

- **Lapsing of health insurance:** Discontinuity in renewal results in both the waiting period and pre-existing disease exclusion period being reset. This is a setback because most claim rejections happen in the waiting period and the sooner one gets past these two to four years, the better. In 2020, the insurance regulator introduced the concept of an eight-year look-back period. This means that after eight years, a health insurance claim cannot be rejected except in case of proven fraud.

- **Lapsing of life insurance:** Surrender or lapse penalties are high. Sometimes you may not even get back the paid premiums. This lowers the already modest returns. However, after a life insurance policy is renewed for three years, claims cannot be rejected.

An issue common to health and life insurance is that if there is a lapse, then the insurer can decide not to issue you the insurance anymore. They will do this if your health has deteriorated since you first bought the insurance or if you have made a claim. But, if you renew on time, the insurer has to renew your insurance.

- **Lapsing of motor insurance:** Motor insurance, a large market segment, have no-claim-bonuses (NCBs) that reduce your premium after every claim-free year, provided there is no break in insurance. You should be possessive about this NCB. The amounts can go up to 65 per cent of own-damage premium and is typically several thousand rupees in most mid-sized cars. You lose your NCB if there is a break in renewal, an expensive proposition.
- **Lapsing of liability insurance:** Professionals, such as doctors, that buy liability insurance lose the retroactive date benefit if there is a break. The retroactive date is the date after which claims get covered. It is when the insurance was first bought, provided you renew the insurance without a break.

The only two individual insurances that do not have benefits accumulating over time, are home insurance and personal accident insurance. In fact, in home insurance you should increase the sum assured every few years, as reconstruction costs increase. Simply renewing your home insurance without making an adjustment in the sum assured is not a good idea.

In personal accident insurance, continuity does not impact any accumulated benefits. This does not mean that you should freely stop and restart any of these insurances. You are not covered for the primary risk when premiums have not been paid.

Insurances lapse for many avoidable reasons. You could have bought the wrong product and decided not to renew. Ideally, this research should be completed before the initial purchase and, in fact, even after making a buy you have a free-look period where you can go through the documentation and return the insurance if you want. Another frequent issue is that insurers cannot contact you. To prevent this make sure you give insurers a permanent email, home address and phone number. Finally, you could lose track of renewals if the insurer or intermediary does not send a reminder. This is also commonplace and we are all guilty of such memory lapses despite having access to elaborate reminders. For several insurances it is now possible to instruct your bank or credit card for automatic renewal. Select those options.

So, the next time an insurer or intermediary chases you to renew, do not procrastinate but make the payment.

Renewal time is an opportunity to switch your insurance if you are not happy with it or if better options have been introduced. This is called porting and can be done without any loss in benefits accumulated. So, how does porting work?

What Does it Mean to Port an Insurance?

Last year two of my friends called to discuss issues regarding porting their insurances. In both cases the facts were similar—they had long-standing health insurances from a public sector insurer. All waiting periods had been completed which meant that even claims pertaining to pre-existing conditions would be paid for. Both friends had then ported their health insurances to a private sector insurer. However, they were in for a surprise when they filed claims in the newly ported insurances. The claims were rejected for non-disclosure of previous ailments. Ideally, this should not have happened because they had already run through the waiting period of their previous insurances.

In health insurance, the waiting period is a maximum of four years, but two to three years is becoming the norm. Additionally, as mentioned above, after eight years of regular renewal, a health insurance claim cannot be rejected except in case of proven fraud. These health insurance features imply that the more you renew your health insurance, the higher the certainty that a claim will be paid.

This may have been a disincentive for people to buy new health insurance products, had it not been for the facility of porting. Porting allows you to switch your health insurance to a new product, provided by any insurer. Porting can be to another product with the same insurer or to a new insurer. In both cases, the insurer being switched to gives credit for the time spent in the previous health insurance by reducing the waiting period in the new product purchased. For example, in the two cases that I described, the new insurer had waived the waiting period completely, because the previous insurances had already run for over five years.

Porting to newer and better insurances is helpful because products are rapidly improving. What you bought a decade ago will most likely be overpriced or outdated. However, do know that porting is only an adjustment of waiting periods. You will be bound by the benefits, exclusions, premiums and contracts of the new health insurance that you buy. Also, insurers are not obliged to accept a porting request. They are entitled to set their own underwriting norms and reject a porting request if they wish.

Practically, many insurers encourage portability by waiving the requirement for additional medical tests or the need to complete detailed forms. They do always ask for a declaration of good health, existence of pre-existing conditions and claims history. An adverse report will result in your porting request being rejected. This makes it important to fully disclose your medical history, even when porting. Porting is not a way to hide medical problems and claim a larger insurance benefit.

The regulator has an inbuilt safeguard to reduce porting-related mis-selling—intermediaries, agents and brokers do not earn a commission on ported insurances. This prevents situations where an intermediary will switch your insurance for their financial gain. The flipside is that intermediaries may not advise you to port an insurance, even if they know better alternatives are available.

If an insurer rejects your porting request, you can still buy a top-up health cover that enhances and adds another layer of insurance over your base plan. These top-ups pay a benefit above a threshold and this makes them more cost-effective than buying regular mediclaim.

Porting also works in motor insurance. However, here it is the NCB that is ported. This NCB can reach 50 per cent (65 per cent in some of the older insurances) of the premium, and is a sizeable amount. Porting motor insurance allows you to retain the premium discount even if you switch insurers for a particular car or buy a new vehicle. You will lose the NCB if your insurance is not renewed on time or if you make a claim.

As I dug deeper into my friends' rejected claims, one claim was turned down because she did not disclose a pre-existing condition, incorrectly assuming that this was not required during porting. For the other friend, the case was curiouser. He was not explicitly asked for a declaration of good health or medical history at all, yet the insurer expected this information. It turned out the ported insurance was forged.

A failed health insurance porting is disastrous for policyholders, because it leaves them uninsured. The previous insurance would have lapsed without a new cover being in place. The most important considerations, then, while porting, are to apply for a port at least a month before renewal, declare your health conditions accurately and close your previous insurance only after the porting request is accepted by the new insurer.

Returning to the example of the fraudulently placed insurance. How common is it? And what can you do to prevent such malpractice?

The Benefit of Due Process

Insurance inhabits two distinct worlds. The first promises concern and care. Search for popular insurance advertisements anywhere in the world and you will find beautiful creatives that bring tears to your eyes. This promise of security is the perspective that I love. However, scratch the surface and a second underworld emerges. One where people have bought the wrong products, felt cheated and struggled to find solutions. This too brings tears, but mostly of frustration. Over the years there have been five different incidents involving close family and friends that brought this second, less attractive world, into the forefront.

- My wife, a surgeon, has been buying professional indemnity insurance for several years from a firm specializing in insurance for doctors. It is a large entity catering to about 30,000 doctors across the country. While reviewing her insurance I was surprised to find that the firm had charged four-times the insurance premium as a fee. The rationale was that premium for three years had been taken upfront and a service fee, roughly equivalent to an annual premium, was being charged.

In my view at least four insurance laws were being violated—the insurance did not have a three-year option so the sale was not valid; premiums have to be deposited with the insurer within twenty-four hours which was not happening; a service fee cannot be bundled with premium; and finally, the company did not appear to be a licensed distributor. I did eventually recover the ₹15,000 additional payment but it was an effort. I wonder if the other 29,999 doctors are aware that they are over-paying, and how they could recover their money.

- In another incident a friend's equipment worth ₹50 lakh burned down. The insurance surveyor said the claim was not payable since it was caused by a faulty switchboard. However, he was willing to give a favourable report for a fee. Should one escalate the matter with the insurer at the risk of not getting any money, or pay the bribe?

- I went car shopping during *shradh* because this inauspicious period has the best discounts, or so I thought. The dealer's price list set insurance premium at ₹45,000. I knew the fair price of that insurance was ₹20,000. So, who checks if premium has been inflated to recover discounts given elsewhere?

- A relative bought fire insurance for their home under construction. Unfortunately, the agent forgot to mention that a standard warranty in the policy was for no construction taking place on the site. That is ₹20,000 burnt up, literally.

- A business colleague's medical claim of ₹5 lakh was declined because the insurer concluded he was drunk when the road accident took place. I am not clear how that decision was made, because the doctor's note and medico-legal report clearly stated that the patient was sober.

How do you address these issues? There are two steps that you must use: follow process and pursue grievances.

- **Processes that allow you to communicate directly with insurers are good**: Fill your form and pay online; if you have an accident, take pictures and email those to the company, communicate with the insurer over email. Verify the policy details when the company's customer care person calls. These simple steps will keep you safe.
- **If you are unhappy about something, a wrongly placed insurance or claim, then meticulously follow the prescribed process.** First escalate the matter within the insurance company and if there is no respite then write to the Insurance Ombudsman. These can both be effective.

  A young girl's father died due to COVID-19 and the insurer settled less than half her claim citing a government notification capping hospital charges. But the capping was only meant for 60 per cent of the beds, and when the young girl pointed this out to the insurer's grievance cell the remaining claim was settled within days.

  Similarly, in another case related to porting, we escalated the matter to the Ombudsman who ruled in favour of the policyholder and the previously rejected claim was paid. There is no substitute to thoroughly following process.

The final test in insurance is when you do eventually make a claim. The refrain amongst insurers is that their reason to exist is to pay claims. Yet, several claims get rejected. Why does this happen and how can you ensure that your claim is not the one that gets rejected?

The Real Reasons Why Claims Get Rejected

You buy insurance expecting claims to be paid and feel bitter when that does not happen. In an ideal world, insurers would communicate terms in easy-to-follow language; buyers would take the time to read what they are buying; documents to file a claim would be simple; and helpful customer service executives would ask for bank details to transfer the claim payment. Nothing is further from reality.

I recently watched Steven Spielberg's *Bridge of Spies* (2015), a film set in the Cold War, about a first-rate insurance lawyer who used his negotiation skills to strike superb deals for the US with Russia and Cuba. How I wish we had such insurance settlement lawyers to represent our insurance buyers. Claim rejection can be high and, until there is a better grievance-handling system, you would do well to understand why. There is little public information on this subject and I draw from experience with hundreds of claims, to list out the main reasons for rejection. Watch out for these in your own insurances.

- **Health insurance claims are denied** because hospitalization was due to an undisclosed pre-existing disease. The fact that a disease is pre-existing gets discovered from the doctor's case history. When insurers are suspicious they ask for the daily hospital and surgical notes as well. These, almost always, bring out the truth because the patient's medical background is captured accurately in them for all the medical staff to refer to. The diseases that are hidden most often are: hypertension (good medication can prevent this from being diagnosed), diabetes (medicine comes to the rescue once again), internal cysts and neurological diseases such as epilepsy.

When a claim is rejected patients get indignant but, often, the subterfuge was deliberate. Where insurers go overboard is in their messianic zeal to classify everything as pre-existing. There are situations where an innocuous comment by the doctor, for example, in listing out a possible differential diagnosis such as 'Sugar?' has resulted in rejection. In many cases the root cause of hospitalization is subjective. For example, was the sharp drop in haemoglobin because of pre-existing piles or newly discovered ulcers? Once the insurer takes a position on this, generally in its own favour, it is hard to convince them otherwise. Life insurance and overseas travel claims are also rejected primarily due to non-disclosure of pre-existing medical problems.

- **In motor insurance, claims are rejected** most often because of negligence. Did you leave the keys in the vehicle? Forget to lock the door? Start the engine when it was flooded? Drive with an expired driver's license? Were drinking and driving? Recently, on Quora, someone asked me the implication of leaving a note on his car saying, 'Steal Me!' and the car gets stolen. Although provocation is not excluded, I doubt if that specific claim will be paid. Insurers look for signs of negligence in police or medico-legal reports. Your description of the accident needs to be consistent for the insurer, surveyor, investigator and anyone else who calls. Another reason for many rejections is that the vehicle is in commercial use, but the insurance is personal.

- **Home insurance claims do not get paid** because of specific exclusions relating to normal wear-and-tear, seepage and short circuits, fires caused by short circuits, and wall damage due to seepage. The other issue with home insurance is that they are incorrectly placed. For example, a basement which is a material risk for insurers, is not declared. Or the fact that a house has been unoccupied is not mentioned. Or there is commercial activity such as keeping paying guests or running small offices on the premises that are not described. A problem that I have encountered is that the person who bought the insurance does not have an insurable interest in the home. For example, a tenant buys building insurance, or the facilities management company in a high-rise buys home insurance rather than the homeowners themselves.

- **Marine insurance covers goods in transit when you relocate or send material elsewhere. These claims are rejected** because standard insurance covers accidents whereas claims often relate to pilferage or damages without an accident. Someone I know was transferring a valuable figurine in a truck. Somewhere along the route the statue disintegrated. The claim was rejected because there was no evidence of an accident. The customer's vivid make-believe portrayal of how the truck driver had to swerve to avoid a collision struck no chord.

- **Burglary claims are rejected** because the buyer did not inform the insurer that the house would be unoccupied for an extended period of time. The second most common issue is that the insurance covers burglary, as in a forced break-in, but not theft, which is an inside job. In any event, many burglary claims go unreported because it is undisclosed cash or gold that is filched. Severe under-insurance, when the value of all your goods is understated to keep premiums low, also results in considerable rejection.

Professionals such as doctors, chartered accountants, architects often buy liability insurances to cover negligence-related litigation. Many service companies are buying cyber insurance to cover for cybercrime. The number of claims filed in these liability insurances is rapidly increasing and it will be interesting to see how often claims get paid in the future. The contracts are stringent and insurers could reject claims. The key here is to describe the scale and nature of your business accurately in the proposal form.

Small businesses buy insurance to cover losses to computers and phones. These claims are denied mainly because the damage is usually caused by negligence. Laptops are the most prone to such denials. Generally, laptops get spoilt because of rough use which is not claimable.

Most of us buy insurances with a single-minded focus on price. Claim rejections can be prevented if we had a single-minded focus on product features instead, such as mediclaim with low waiting periods, home insurance with an accurate description of structure and contents, marine insurance that covers all risks rather than just accidents. These cost more but make the insurance meaningful.

My focus here has been on rejected claims. There is equally valuable information embedded in paid claims. For example, in 2015 a leading cause of claims was children's injuries on trampolines. In Delhi, these 'bouncies' are ubiquitous at birthday parties. Now, finally, I have a rational reason to forbid children from clambering on to them.

There is one area where claims settlement is indisputably high and that is on death. This is a reassuring reason to buy term covers. And it is instructive to understand why these claims get settled so efficiently.

The Sterling Track Record of Life Insurers in Paying Claims

Recently, I read some opinions that expressed concern about low death-claims payment in life insurance. This view is one reason some hesitate to buy life insurance. Nothing could be further from the truth. Claims payment in life insurance is extremely high and several regulatory provisions ensure this.

In 2020–21, over 2.1 million death claims were paid in India. Fewer than 17,000 claims, a minute fraction of those paid, were rejected. One reason is that, by law, life insurance can have no exclusions, except suicide in the first year of purchase. This was not always the case. About fifteen years ago, it was routine for life insurances to exclude death for certain reasons in the initial insurance period. This has now been abandoned in all products. The only thing that buyers must be careful about is the difference between life and personal accident insurance. Both pay an amount on death, but whereas life insurance covers death by any cause, personal accident insurance covers only accident-related death. Personal accident insurance also has various exclusions such as death due to risky activities or by substance abuse. These exclusions, however, are not allowed in life insurance. In other words, life insurance would cover death due to risky activities or by substance abuse.

In a life insurance claim, you just need to establish that the insured person has died and a death certificate is the primary document for that.

Claims can be rejected only if a buyer deliberately hides information when filling the proposal form. This is not uncommon and, typically, the information hidden relates to poor health and other insurances that a person has already bought. Both these bits of information are necessary for insurers to properly underwrite the insurance. Adverse health indicates less longevity and an excessive amount of insurance is a red flag for insurers to look into. Recent court judgements, including in the Supreme Court, have clarified that non-disclosure of all required information when buying the insurance is ground for declining a claim.

However, rejections on the ground of non-disclosure, are going to become more difficult because of the provision that a life insurance claim cannot be rejected after three years of the policy start date. The rationale is that three years is a long time and it is unfair to link death after this period to deliberate ill intent on the part of a buyer. These regulations ensure that life insurance death claims get paid. This three-year stipulation is a strong incentive to buy life insurance early, because claim rejections become so much harder with time.

Not only do claims get paid, but there are also regulations to ensure that they get paid fast. The Protection of Policyholder Interest 2017 regulations require that in death claims, all documentation requirements be raised simultaneously, rather than piecemeal, within fifteen days of intimation. Also, a claims decision, even if investigation is needed, must be made within ninety days of intimation. Payments then have to be made within thirty days of the decision.

In case of delays, insurers must pay an interest of 2 per cent over the current bank rate. This would be about 6.25 per cent today. The interest paid on account of settlement delays as well as claim settlement periods are reported and actively discussed by insurers in their boards and policyholder-protection committees. The implication for you is that insurers need to quickly settle death claims. About 99 per cent of the claims pending on 31 March 2021, had been pending for less than six months. And the reason for delay is most often that claimants have not sent all the details they that were asked for.

Once you have bought life insurance the insurer must renew it each year for the term you selected, even if your health worsens. There is a grace period of thirty days after the renewal date to make your payment, except in monthly payments where the grace period is fifteen days.

If you do not renew within time then your insurance lapses. In the first six months after a lapse, insurers will generally reinstate your insurance at your request, with just a declaration of good health. However, after six months, they can refuse to renew or charge you more. The essence is that you must buy term insurance as early as possible, ideally when you start working, without worrying about claim settlement. And then renew your insurance punctually each year.

But what about health insurance, particularly COVID-19 claims? Have these been paid?

Why Covid Claims Are Only Partially Settled

There are two dichotomous perspectives on the payment of COVID-19 health insurance claims. One narrative blames insurers for not paying enough claims, the other castigates hospitals for gouging profits. Both narratives are flawed and the truth is more nuanced.

I pulled out at random, thirty recent COVID-19 health insurance claims. Of these, twenty-six were paid and four rejected. In the twenty-six paid claims, the average claim size was ₹2 lakh but average claim settled was ₹1.4 lakh or 70 per cent of the hospital bill. This means that insurers deducted 30 per cent of the hospital bill for a variety of reasons. The deduction across the twenty-six claims was not uniform. In eighteen of the twenty-six cases, the deduction was less than 30 per cent, in four cases the reduction was between 30–50 per cent, and in four cases over 50 per cent. Deductions of up to 30 per cent are routine and mostly linked to specific policy coverages and disallowed items. So, my focus is on the eight cases where deduction was high, and of course on the four COVID-19 cases that were rejected.

Mostly, the high deductions were fair and because of the insurance policy's terms and conditions. For example, some insurances had a cap on hospital room rent that was breached because patients opted for higher room categories that gave them more isolation and privacy. In some of these insurances the buyers had opted for a co-pay of 10–20 per cent and that co-pay was correctly deducted. Similarly, insurers have rejected the payment of items such as oximeters, oxygen purchases, BIPAP machines because these are outside covered items. Finally, some deductions were made for the fixed discount that hospitals are meant to give insurers. This is fair and the hospital would not have charged the patient for this.

In some cases, claim deductions were made because the hospital tariff was not in line with either the general insurance council guidelines or recommendations of statutory bodies like state governments. This issue is more complicated. If the rates were recommended by government bodies with authority over the hospital and those rates are being violated then the hospital is at fault and rate enforcement is needed. If the rates recommended by the general insurance council have been breached then the question is whether the general insurance council, a body that represents insurers, has the right to set hospital rates?

Irrespective of whether the hospital or insurer is at fault, the cost is borne by you. The only way to regulate this is for the statutory bodies and governments to set and enforce treatment rates that are fair to all. This issue extends beyond the room tariff to the cost and usage of PPEs, masks and other equipment. In the claims there were deductions for excess usage of PPEs. But this is not something that you have any control on. Similarly, in Delhi we have seen usurious cost of oxygen concentrators and critical medicines. This area has been largely unregulated. In the absence of reasonable guidelines these costs get deducted in a claim. Finally, another grey area is the treatment protocol for COVID-19. Some of the deductions were for use of drugs or treatment considered experimental. In fact, the protocols themselves have been changing rapidly. In the early days, hydroxychloroquine was considered a prophylactic. No more. Plasma therapy and ivermectin are still in the grey area. This is another example of costs where you have no say, but have to bear the brunt.

Finally, on claims that were denied, the reason given by insurers was that hospitalization was unnecessary. But such an argument wrongly assumes that you want to get hospitalized and hospitals are willing accomplices. This may be true in other ailments but not in COVID-19. Few will willingly take the unnecessary risk of going to a hospital and getting exposed further, and hospitals are struggling to accommodate people from a long waiting list.

In one Gurugram hospital that I am familiar with, the parking lot was being used to hold beds, a guest house was rented and the hospital worked round the clock to get people discharged. They do not want more patients. In such claim rejections the insurer must have stronger reasons. If these patients were to approach the Insurance Ombudsman, their claims would most likely be paid because hospitalization is considered a medical not an insurance decision.

Eventually, the system would work best if everyone focused on their own jobs—insurers set policy features and pricing, governments set and monitored hospital charges, and doctors set treatment protocols.

If you have a COVID-19 claim where you believe the decision or deduction is unfair, write to the insurer's grievance cell. They are sensitive to Covid-related complaints. Recently, a friend passed away from COVID-19. The total hospital bill was about ₹60,000 but the insurer reimbursed only ₹30,000, citing a Delhi Government restriction on room tariff. When we looked at the government notification carefully it stated that the fixed rates were applicable to only 60 per cent of the beds. The notification was silent on the remaining 40 per cent beds. When this was politely pointed out to the insurer's grievance cell they paid the remaining claim amount within forty-eight hours. A fact-based complaint is more effective than threatening protests.

Things do sometimes go wrong in your insurance. The policy copy may have errors or you may want some changes or a claim may be unfairly turned down or, as in the example above, the proper amount may not have been paid. What can you do in such cases? How do you ensure a fair hearing?

Perseverance Pays When it Comes to Claims

Some years ago, *The New Yorker* released a curated edition of its best cartoons over the past ninety years. My favourite is of two cavemen who have obviously just made a sacrificial offering. One of them looks quizzically at the other and says, 'I don't know how the gods feel, but sacrificing financial advisers makes me feel happy.' I could not help chuckling even though the joke is on people like me—advisers in finance, insurance and other such fields. Every morning I get a google alert for the words 'insurance broker'. The typical news headlines are 'Insurance broker sentenced to four years in prison', 'Insurance broker scams truckers', and so on.

The criticism of insurance is severe because of mis-selling, poor complaint-handling related to claims and tardy servicing. Much has been said about mis-selling so I will let that be. Poor complaint-handling causes considerable reputation damage. The general process is to write to the insurer a few times, then to IRDAI, and finally to the Insurance Ombudsman. Each step has its limitations but perseverance yields results.

According to IRDAI there were 684 unresolved grievances in the fiscal year 2018–19, whereas 207,188 complaints were resolved. That is a resolution rate of 99.7 per cent. This 99.7 per cent is misleading because it includes cases where the insurer, against whom the complaint was made in the first place, tells the complainer that their complaint is not valid. That is a conflict of interest. In the fiscal year 2020–21, the grievances attended were 201,617 but we do not know the outcome.

The level of dissatisfaction is certainly higher than what the data suggests. In the hundred or so individual health insurance claims that I have seen at close quarters, over half were initially rejected by the insurer. Many for frivolous reasons—a claim, after a child was hospitalized for observation because of heightened seizure risk, was refused payment because no procedure was done on the child; a woman admitted for angina pain was turned down because the insurer felt that women were less susceptible to heart attacks; the claim filed after the death of a senior citizen due to liver cirrhosis was rejected because the underwriter was convinced that cirrhosis could only have been caused by alcoholism; a claim following an internal cyst removal procedure in a forty-five-year-old lady was rejected because the cyst would have existed before she bought the insurance, even though she was not aware of its existence. The common thread in these cases is that when escalated to senior personnel within the insurance company, the claims were paid. Not as a favour, but because they were legitimately payable.

What can you do if you do not have such privileged access to the higher-ups? Well, you can complain to IRDAI's grievance handling cell but they will only redirect the complaint to the insurance company once again, because the IRDAI does not adjudicate claims. However, claims redirected by the IRDAI are carefully looked into by the insurance company.

You can also complain to the Insurance Ombudsman. Do keep in mind that a claim filed with the Ombudsman can take long to resolve and you have to diligently follow it up. In a recent case, we've had to submit documents multiple times and at one point the Ombudsman threatened to transfer the case from Delhi to Chandigarh because the complainant lived in Gurugram which is in Haryana. Courts are the last resort but they are already overworked and may take years to resolve such cases.

Tardy servicing is a less recognized problem but also causes considerable issues. Servicing is the process of issuing insurance with all the details correctly recorded, answering queries promptly and accurately, and making endorsements fast. It sounds simple, but is not. I routinely get home insurances with the insured address wrong (it is amazing how many different ways 'Bubbles', a house name, can be misspelt); health insurances with incorrect details of pre-existing diseases (for example, joint pain was excluded, although the buyer had specified lower-back pain; and pre-existing asthma dropped from the insurance contract); and cases of renewal reminders not delivered.

Email responses can be long-winded and unhelpful. In one harrowing incident the insurer kept asking the claimant for a scanned document, despite the claimant repeatedly pointing out that this was attached to the original email. Call centres can be bureaucratic. It is difficult for me to get the fund value for my wife's insurance from the call centre if I reveal my true identity. But if I introduce myself as Mrs Mehta the job gets done fast!

Until all these issues get sorted out what can you do if caught on the wrong side of an insurance complaint? If your intention is to unfairly make money from insurance, just give up. It will not work. However, if you have a genuine issue then do not give up. Do not rant, but calmly explain your perspective. A logical case is most compelling. Keep escalating the matter—first within the insurance company, then the IRDAI and lastly the Insurance Ombudsman, in that order—until you are satisfied. Legitimate claims will eventually get paid.

Taking care of your insurances is a continuous process. Every few years you ought to look at your insurance portfolio. There will always be new insurances to buy, but also important are insurances that you need to let go of. Which insurances are those likely to be?

Spring Cleaning Your Insurances

Friends often send me their insurance portfolios to review. As I browse through the dusty files there are many insurances that are no longer relevant. Much like the lives and assets they insure, insurances grow old, get ravaged by time and are made redundant by circumstances. Insurances do not last forever. You must occasionally review and clean up your insurances, sometimes just letting them go.

Insurances can become irrelevant because of product improvements. Our insurance history has a few such examples.

- **Unit-Linked Insurance Plans:** Many continue to hold ULIPs that were issued before October 2010. These plans are characterized by high administrative and fund management charges, both upfront and ongoing. It was not unusual for over half the premium, in those early ULIPs, to be deducted in the first year itself. As I review those insurances today, all of which have been in force for over ten years, the accumulated fund is often just slightly higher than the premium paid. This suggests that significant value has been destroyed. Had the premiums been invested in fixed deposits the accumulated fund would have been 1.5 times the premium.

  In October 2010, the IRDAI stipulated a limit on the charges in ULIPs. Overnight, the product improved dramatically.

  But what of the purchases made before October 2010? Those have continued and, in many cases, the surrender charge is now minimal. If you have insurances like that it may make sense to replace those with the newer products or invest elsewhere.

- **Term plans:** They were introduced in India around 2001. Initially, these were not popular because agents, the primary distributors, earned little when they sold term insurance. However many early adopters, did buy these plans. Now it is time for those pioneers to replace their old term covers with new term plans.

  In the previous ten years, term insurance rates have fallen significantly because the online channel has made price comparison easy and the industry now has better mortality data. So, if you bought a term plan over five years ago it is possible you will save money by buying new plans today, even after adjusting for the fact that you will pay rates for an older age. You could choose not to save money, instead increasing your sum assured within the same budget. Either way, let go of the old plan.

- **Stand-alone critical-illness plans:** General and health insurers have adopted the critical illness innovation and launched stand-alone critical-illness plans that cost-effectively cover more diseases—often over twenty—with higher sums assured and lifelong renewability.

  An early innovation around 2003 in life insurance was to sell riders attached to the base insurance plan. The critical illness rider, in particular, was valuable because health insurance options were limited back then. The rider paid a fixed benefit if the insured person developed pre-specified critical illnesses—typically four to eight diseases. A decade later those old critical illness riders are less relevant in the face of the standalone and cost-effective critical-illness plans.

Perfectly good insurances get destroyed by inflation. Mediclaim insurances bought before 2010 were of small sums assured, less than ₹5 lakh, they did not have a provision to increase the sum assured, and had several other restrictions. Today, such insurances have become inadequate for even basic hospitalization or room rent costs. If you rely only on these old mediclaim policies, out-of-pocket expenses will be high. Consider buying a new health insurance with higher sum assured and fewer restrictions. Port your old insurances so that you get the benefit of shorter waiting periods.

- **Home insurance:** Early adopters of home insurance bought a certain sum assured that was adequate to cover insurance costs a decade ago. Today those sums assured are much less than actual construction costs. The extent of under-insurance over a ten-year period can be as high as 50 per cent. In home insurance claims, payments are reduced by the extent of under-insurance. This means that only half the claim amount will be paid if you suffer a loss today. Replace this insurance with a new home insurance that has the correct sum assured; over-insure so that your insurance remains relevant for some time to come.

- **Asset insurance:** Some asset insurances such as computer-all-risk also lose value over time. That is because the sum assured is linked to the depreciated value of computers, which is well below replacement cost after two or three years.

Insurances can be made redundant by changes in law or, in some cases, by the absence of expected change. Several years ago, income-tax laws were modified to give tax-free status to only those insurances where the sum assured was more than ten times the premium paid. If you have an old insurance that does not meet this condition then it is time to change that, provided surrender charges are reasonable. Pension plans have an issue because the expected tax exemptions for annuities did not materialize. According to current law, annuities are treated as income and taxed. This reduces the effective return on annuities to about 5–6 per cent, well below inflation, if you are in a high tax bracket. So, take a relook at the pension plans in your portfolio as well.

There are other reasons why you may need to discard an insurance. For example, if you buy term insurance, then an accidental death cover is less relevant because that risk is covered by term plans. Sudden changes in wealth also requires a portfolio relook because your financial security requirements change.

Such a clean-up is not something you need to do each year, once in five years is more reasonable. And what better time to start than now.

Buying good insurance reduces your stress about an unpredictable future. You must, however, always read your insurances carefully. This prevents surprises later. What specifically should you scrutinize?

Check. Verify. Reconfirm.

Every once in a while, someone in our company gets an email from my official account asking them to immediately transfer money to a third-party bank account. These are phishing emails, where someone impersonates me to steal. Cybercrimes have increased during the pandemic. Recently, 130 twitter accounts of prominent personalities were hacked and about USD 120,000 stolen. Not all crimes are digital though. Last year a friend's health claim was rejected for non-disclosure, because the sales team had hidden his ill-health from the insurer.

Insurance buyers often describe unkept promises. In life insurance, the most common are: the promise of a high return, 15 per cent or more; the assurance that only a few premiums need be paid; the understanding that in a pension plan, funds can be withdrawn at will; and a guarantee that buying insurance makes you eligible for a loan.

In health insurance, the broken promises include: pre-existing health conditions covered immediately, even if not declared, and all continuity benefits have been protected when you buy a new insurance. Fewer promises would be broken if buyers verified information more diligently. There are many regulatory safeguards and diligence is easy.

The main diligence document in life insurance is the sales illustration. It is mandatory for insurers to get it signed by you and send a copy of it with your policy. The illustration lists out your premium payments over the years and outlines possible returns. The interest rate range that these illustrations generally show is 4–8 per cent. Since these are the returns that the insurer earns, your returns will be lower. The 4–8 per cent band is carefully selected to set reasonable expectations. A promise of higher return is not credible. This illustration also details the amount you can withdraw each year, if you surrender the insurance.

In health insurance, the main documents to review are the proposal form and your policy itself. Both will be sent by the insurer as standard practice. The proposal form outlines the information that has been shared with the insurer by the salesperson or you; and this information has formed the basis of underwriting. Any verbal discussion beyond this form is not considered. The policy has details of continuity benefits, records of dates of birth, and pre-existing conditions that have been noted. These two documents let you know if the insurer is aware of your pre-existing health conditions and if your waiting periods are over.

Some buyers would like to get more details about an insurer. Specifically: their claim settlement, complaint and grievance rates, and financial strength. These can be determined from public disclosures that each insurer publishes quarterly on their websites. For a life insurance policy read Form L-22 on analytical ratios in the public disclosure, this has the insurer's performance on sales, net worth, persistency and investment returns. Forms L-39 to 41 have excellent information on claims and grievances. For health insurance the equivalent forms to read are NL-24, 25, 30 and 41.

To verify the credentials of the person selling you insurance you must know whether they are an individual agent, web-aggregator, corporate agent, broker or some other approved entity. Ask for an ID if you can and communication from their official emails. Insurers put up a list of terminated agents on their websites. And, the insurance regulator publishes the list of active corporate agents, brokers, web aggregators and other distributors on its website (https://www.irdai.gov.in). Other reliable sources of information are www.policyholder. gov.in for policyholder information, www.gicouncil.in which is the general insurance council's website, www.lifeinscouncil.org which is the life insurance council's website and www.ibai.org which is the insurance brokers' association website.

Other good practices are to drop a message to the insurers' support and helpdesk sites with any of your doubts. They will respond, but even if they do not, the fact that you shared your understanding with the insurer is useful if there is a dispute. Insurers make a welcome call in many cases after you have bought an insurance. This is another opportunity for you get clarification. I have seen situations where the welcome caller clarified, and the customer acknowledged, that the insurance was no guarantee of a loan. Yet a few months later the customer complained of a broken promise.

More direct questioning, insistence on written responses and your own research through verified sources will prevent surprises.

PART 3

Insurance Documents

8

Understanding the Fine Print

MY DAUGHTER IS studying law and sometimes shares her assignments with me. As I read her work, I am filled with confidence that she has a secure future. She is good at what she does, of course, but it's equally important that there is no way a layperson can navigate the dense fog of legalese in the various documents and case laws. A lawyer will always be needed to interpret these documents.

This legalese is an issue in insurance because the contracts are drawn up by insurers with a deep understanding of law, and the implications are on policyholders like you, that have no option but to accept the terms. Consider these cases:

- A critical illness exclusion in the contract of a leading insurer says:

Critical Illness symptom/s (and / or the treatment) of which were present in the insured person at any time before inception of this policy or on the date on which cover here under was granted to such insured person, or which manifests itself within a period of three calendar months from such date, whether or not the insured or the insured person has knowledge that the symptoms or treatment were related to such Critical Illness.

Translated, this means: We will not pay a claim if the disease began before you bought this insurance. Whether you knew it or not.

- A few years ago, my daughter was diagnosed with a tapeworm infection. The paediatric neurosurgeon recommended hospitalization for two days to initiate treatment. The oral medicine to kill the tapeworms sometimes causes seizures, and hospitalization allows immediate action. My health insurer pre-approved this hospitalization, but when the time to pay came, they backed out because in their view, hospitalization was not required. The insurance contract had a clause that specified that 'medical expenses where in-patient care is not warranted' would not be reimbursed.
- A company bought COVID-19 insurance for all its employees because the insurance covered home treatment. When dozens of claims were rejected, the company saw a note in the contract that said home care would be covered if there was no place in hospitals or the doctor specified that the patient was in no condition to move.
- A doctor bought property insurance for her clinic. The insurer, in the policy copy, introduced a 24-hour security warranty that required her clinic to have a security guard at

all times. In this case, the doctor noticed the insertion and had it removed.

This section describes ambiguity in insurance contracts as well as contractual requirements that you may have to fulfil for an insurance. While it may take time for the ambiguity to reduce, you should take comfort in the fact that the regulator and courts strongly encourage insurers to interpret policy contracts in favour of policyholders and claimants.

The Safeguards in Your Insurance

About twelve years ago, a sixty-five-year-old gentleman, visited me. After paying premium for eight years, he had been informed that his medical insurance would not be renewed. Despite having read the contract, he'd missed noticing the clause that restricted the maximum age to sixty-five. Now, given his worsening hypertension, the man feared that no insurer would cover him.

There are two distinct approaches to writing laws for financial products. The democratic way is to put out detailed disclosures and then leave customers to make their choices. The other, more authoritarian, route is to build safeguards into the law such that even if a financially illiterate person (an overwhelming majority) were to buy the insurance they would be okay. Any law is a mix of these two approaches. But I find mandatory safeguards more effective than disclosures.

Health insurance has some excellent safeguards. All health covers now must be renewable lifelong. The sixty-five-year-old gentleman I wrote about is now seventy-seven, and would still have had his original health insurance if this legislation had come in earlier. The law also stipulates that the premium you pay should be in line with the entire class of people your age. Insurers are not allowed to charge you a different rate just because you made a claim. These two features, put together, make it imperative that you buy insurance early on, when you are healthy, and then hold on to it for life.

The law, in 2013, standardized the definitions of several exclusions and diseases. All insurers now follow these defined terms for things such as pre-existing diseases, cancer, room rent, and hospitals. Previously, for example, pre-existing diseases were interpreted in many ways. Some said that the policyholder should be aware of the disease, others that awareness is not necessary. The time of pre-existing symptoms also varied widely. With the current safeguard, even if you do not read the contract, a minimum standard will be adhered to.

The law now excludes health insurance from the principle of contribution. This contribution clause stipulated that if you have multiple insurances then each insurer must pay their proportionate share of a claim. This sometimes led to delayed payments and disputes. For example, one insurer would accept the claim and the other might reject. Or in cases of cashless claims, there would be disputes about which insurer should pay first and up to what limit. Today, you can decide which insurer to approach and they will have to pay the entire amount, subject to their insurance's sum assured limits.

Previously, claims had to be submitted within a certain number of days, typically thirty to sixty days. The restriction still holds but the regulations ask insurers to condone delays if there is a reasonable cause.

Life insurance also has many safeguards. The only claim that will not be paid for is suicide in the first policy year. As discussed earlier, claims cannot be repudiated after the insurance has been in force for three years. These conditions effectively shift the responsibility of identifying issues of misrepresentation or non-disclosure to the insurer and set a time limit for such discovery.

In ULIPs the yield reduction allowed is capped. In these products you decide which assets to invest in. The yield-reduction cap limits the charges in your insurance and assures that the returns you get are in line with the underlying assets. An insurer cannot pay excessive commissions or charge you high fees, because that will breach the allowed reduction in yield. Another excellent safeguard is that there cannot be a surrender charge if you close your insurance after five years. This benefit goes hand in hand with the restriction that you cannot withdraw money in the first five years. So, the law forces you to take at least a five-year outlook when you invest in a ULIP.

Life and health insurance allow a free-look period of fifteen to thirty days to return your insurance if you're not satisfied. Similarly, a thirty-day renewal grace period is inbuilt so that you do not lose continuity benefits if you miss your renewal but pay within thirty days of the due date.

There are some areas where safeguards are not strong enough. Traditional participating endowments, the largest selling life insurance, do not have limits on charges and surrender costs similar to ULIPs. Some definitions, across insurances, are unclear. For example, exclusion due to substance abuse is not specific. The difference between external and internal congenital diseases causes confusion. The free-look period and thirty-day grace period concept does not extend to property and liability insurance.

There is a silver lining to the story about the man who lost his insurance at sixty-five. The market has developed so much over the past few years that he has been able to buy, even with his hypertension, a new and better insurance with a higher sum assured. This time all the safeguards have been automatically built in.

In insurance, the laws protect your interests. Over the course of the past few years, these have become even more policyholder-friendly. Understanding these laws better will put you at ease. What are they and how do they protect you?

How Regulations Have Your Back

In 2019, several new regulations were introduced. These consisted of many seemingly incremental changes but when put together become a meaningful step forward for policyholders. The regulations cover life insurance, both traditional and unit-linked (ULIP), health insurance, TPAs, fixed-benefit critical-illness and personal accident plans, insurance distributors and a framework for product innovation.

The focus of the life-insurance law was to encourage innovation in pure-risk term plans and find product solutions to reduce the high lapse rates. In term insurance, insurers can now issue policies for even one month. Previously, less than a year was not allowed. Insurers have responded by launching low-value term plans for specific purposes such as credit-card outstandings. Term plans are comprehensive and with fewer restrictions than personal accident insurances currently available for short terms. In these regulations, the issue of high lapses is partly addressed by increasing the reinstatement period, when a lapsed policy can be revived with just a declaration of good health, from two to five years in traditional plans and to three years in ULIPs. A reason for lapse is that policyholders can no longer afford to pay. In new products, insurers can offer an option to reduce premium by 50 per cent after five years. Finally, insurers may now collect renewal premium three months before the due date compared to the previous rule of thirty days. This allows insurers to begin the renewal effort well ahead of due dates. These changes address the product flexibility needed to reduce lapses, but mis-selling issues will also need to be addressed.

There are other areas where positive steps have been taken. In ULIPs there was an overall limit on total charges. Now, caps on individual charges have also been introduced.

In health insurance a committee report that restricts exclusions was published and final regulations subsequently notified. The provisions implemented are policyholder-friendly. Specifically, a look-back period of eight years has been introduced, the definition of pre-existing diseases changed, and diseases contracted after buying an insurance covered.

A look-back means that after eight years a claim cannot be rejected unless a fraud is proven. There is a similar rule in life insurance where claims may not be rejected after three years. A frequent reason for rejecting claims is that the medical condition existed before the insurance was bought. The previous definition allowed insurers to classify ailments as pre-existing even if symptoms existed, but the disease was not diagnosed. Now, a condition can be classified pre-existing only if the medical condition has been diagnosed or treated before. Finally, diseases contracted after buying insurance, including illnesses, such as Alzheimer's, Parkinson's or HIV/AIDS, cannot be excluded.

The health insurance changes have prohibited the use of ambiguous phrases such as 'directly or indirectly related', or 'such as'. This will require insurance lawyers to brush up their writing skills. I am myself guilty of using the phrase 'such as' seven times in this chapter! Chronic conditions such as hypertension or diabetes will not be allowed a waiting period of over thirty days and some exclusions, that previously existed, such as oral chemotherapy and peritoneal dialysis are no longer allowed.

A proposed guideline will allow critical-illness or personal accident insurances to pay the sum assured in instalments. This feature reduces the possibility of surviving family members squandering an insurance benefit. In health insurance, some insurers outsource claim handling to TPAs. A proposed regulation allows buyers to select a TPA of their choice.

An announcement in the 2018 Budget was the decision to allow 100 per cent foreign direct investment (FDI), up from 49 per cent, in insurance intermediaries, including brokers, surveyors and web aggregators. This was subsequently notified. Investment is most likely in individual health and life insurance and this in turn will provide buyers more options. The regulators have also issued a regulatory sandbox guideline that will allow companies to try out innovative ideas, even if they do not fall within the current regulatory framework. This initiative is now in the second cycle.

With all these changes, now is a suitable time to review your insurance portfolio and make sure that health, life and accident risks are covered. Another source of comfort for you should be that in cases of litigation, the courts overwhelmingly favour policyholders. Read on for one such example.

How Courts Favour Policyholders

In February 2018, Hon'ble Judge Pratibha Singh of the Delhi High Court, issued a judgement in the United India Insurance versus Jai Parkash Tayal case.[52] The issue at stake was that Mr Tayal's claim for a heart condition was rejected on the grounds of being a genetic disorder. He had bought his health insurance in 2004 and had been paid claims twice, in 2004 and 2006, for the same heart condition. The third time a claim was made in 2011, the insurer rejected it because an exclusion for genetic conditions had been introduced in the contract in 2010, the seventh policy year.

The high court ruled that the claim be paid, and the rationale behind it has been elegantly outlined in a forty-seven-page judgement. This is one of the finest orders I have read and examines the matter from multiple perspectives, including international and domestic laws, constitutional principles, public law, nature of contract, disease aetiology and potential implications.

A crucial point made in the judgement is that the insurance contract is one-sided. This one-sidedness comes about because insurance buyers have no ability to modify the agreement. You can reject the insurance, which is not realistic because other insurers have similar contracts, or just accept it in totality. The judgement argues, correctly, that given this one-sided nature, the contract terms must be fair, reasonable and constitutional.

Even if you have explicitly accepted the contract, the terms can be disputed if they are unfair. The implications of this principle extend to many areas in the insurance purchase process. For example, the government had mandated that all insurance policies be linked to Aadhaar cards by 31 March 2018. Claims would not be paid if this linkage was incomplete. This one-sided diktat created stress. The process would not get done on time because in many cases customers would not have submitted Aadhaar cards and, in others, the insurers would not have done the linkages properly in their systems. This is an example of a requirement, unilaterally introduced by one party, where the claimant has no choice but to comply. This requirement was subsequently waived.

Another significant point made in the judgement is that of the insurer unilaterally changing exclusions in the policy contract during annual renewals. When a health insurance is bought for the first time, you study the options carefully. Subsequently, on renewal, you do not review the insurance again because the implicit assumption is that the insurance cover will remain unchanged over the years. That is not the case, however, because in the case of United Insurance versus Tayal, a new exclusion was introduced seven years after the initial policy was bought. And it was this new exclusion that resulted in the claim being rejected, even though two claims of a similar nature had already been paid before.

I pulled out, at random, the policy wordings of a popular health insurance product in 2014 and compared that to the wordings used by the same product in 2018. There were seven new permanent exclusion clauses that had been added in the four years.

The new exclusions included select laser treatments, high-intensity ultrasounds, Cyberknife treatments, bio-absorbable stents, Parkinson's and Alzheimer's even if aggravated by an accident, genetic disorders, stem-cell surgeries, taking part in military exercises, aviation in professional or semi-professional capacities, oral chemotherapy, use of Remicade or Avastin unless in IPD, and accidents due to hazardous activities. These hazardous activities included, amongst many others, trekking and martial arts. That put an end to my children's Krav Maga classes. Also, newly included, was a list of hospitals from where claims would not be allowed.

Not all changes were detrimental to policyholders. For example, the exclusion on internal congenital diseases was removed. However, modifying the contract on renewal creates uncertainty about what will be covered in the future. You cannot easily shift to other insurers because of the effort and possible loss of continuity benefits.

The third matter that the judgement highlighted was the need for specificity in exclusions. The issue, they pointed out, in excluding genetic disorders is that these are ambiguous. In the case at hand, four expert witnesses had different interpretations on the degree to which the heart disorder was genetic. Therefore sweeping, subjective exclusions should be removed as far as possible. An example is the 'war' exclusion common across insurers. In some cases, there are over twelve synonyms used for war which include civil war, detentions, commotions, capture, restraint, arrests, detainment, hostilities and insurrections. More on this ambiguity in the next chapter.

The high court judgement brings out some prominent issues that go beyond insurance. One of these is the right to privacy. If genetic tests are carried out to understand disease aetiology then claimants would be exposed to information leaks. A person with genes suggestive of serious illness could be denied insurance, jobs or marriage. The information does leak out, as we have seen with motor insurances, where your personal information is widely available.

It took six years for this case to be adjudicated. There are no public numbers easily available but I estimate the number of insurance-specific litigations to be over 30,000. This could come down if exclusions are made more specific and remain unchanged on renewal.

It must not have been pleasant for the insurer to be at the receiving end of Justice Singh's comments. At one point in the judgement, the hon'ble judge berated the insurer for refusing to honour a claim based on a broad understanding, and then added the words '*or misunderstanding*' in italics to emphasize the mistake. That must have made Mr Tayal smile.

A considerable number of grievances and litigations are due to insurance contracts that are ambiguous. This is an area that the regulator and insurers are steadily improving, but it is important for you to understand the nuances. What is the ambiguity that causes the most issues?

Insurance Contracts are One-Sided and Ambiguous. But That Should Not Worry You

Over the past few years several people have complained to me about their insurance contracts. Often these contracts have vague conditions and include clauses that are patently unfair to policyholders. Since buyers receive the policy contract at the end of a long sales process, they typically do not have the energy to reopen a discussion with insurers. Even if they did, I doubt if they would make much headway. In a few cases, I did attempt to modify or clarify a contract. Unfortunately, I have not yet met with much success. The policy contract is considered non-negotiable. As a result, customers are left with an uneasy feeling that their claims will be dismissed on technicalities and legalese.

Let me share some common issues. A particularly malfeasant clause in health and travel insurance used to be that 'claims can be denied if the policyholder fails to seek or follow medical advice'. What exactly did that mean? What diseases should a policyholder seek medical advice for? What if he felt that advice was not needed and the problem was routine? After all, most serious diseases begin with some basic symptoms. What if the policyholder took two opinions and disregarded one? Fortunately, this exclusion was prohibited in 2019.[53]

With a private sector life insurer, we ran into the odd situation of inconsistent exclusions in the base term insurance policy and the accidental death rider. The only exclusion in the base term life cover was suicide in the first policy year. However, the accidental rider excluded suicide in all years. The customer hesitated to clarify this with the insurer because she felt the insurer would interpret her question as an intention to commit suicide, after the first policy year, and cancel her policy!

We sought clarification on her behalf and were quite astonished when the insurer confirmed the inconsistent exclusions.

A common issue is the generic, catch-all nature of questions asked in proposal forms. One such question is: 'Have you undergone any tests or investigations or been advised to undergo any tests or investigations?' Unless one has grown up on a diet of Kryptonite the answer to this question will always be 'yes'. Most of you would pass this question off as a bureaucratic query and respond in the negative. Does this mean that an insurer can say that information has been misrepresented in the proposal form and decline your claim? What is the material level at which an investigation should be reported?

Corporate insurances have similar problems. Most group contracts allow the insurer to cancel the policy at any time without a penalty. For example, if seven months into an annual group health policy the claims are too high, an insurer can refund the remaining five months of premium and terminate the contract. This puts the insured company at considerable risk if claims shoot up. The rules work differently when the insured company wants to cancel a policy and a severe financial penalty is imposed.

Insurance is not a tangible product but a promise by an insurer to pay claims. It is imperative that the promise be specific with minimal caveats. This is the direction in which insurance contracts have been moving.

Ambiguous, one-sided contracts are not something that you can do much about, but you should take comfort in the fact that the regulator and courts are actively pro-policyholder and interpret the contracts in a way that benefits you.

There are two reasons why contracts can be ambiguous. The first is that the insurer wants to leave the door open for interpretation. The second, more pervasive, is just poor drafting skills and the fact that many contracts are cut-and-paste jobs of other contracts. How should you read and interpret content that is difficult to understand?

The Role of Mindfulness When Reading the Policy Contract

Just before the pandemic began, I had walked past an office that displayed a large, attractive poster advocating 'Say No to Single-Use Plastic' printed on single-use plastic. Such thoughtlessness is pervasive, but if it takes place in insurance the impact can be significant. That is because insurance is not a tangible product but a promise to pay claims in the future, sometimes decades later. If the insurance product is not clear it can result in you accepting terms, conditions and warranties without realizing the possible impact on claims.

One reason for apparent thoughtlessness is ambiguous language. My own health insurance, a very good purchase, says on the opening page that 'This policy certificate is to be read with the policy wordings, as one contract or any word or expression to which a specific meaning has been attached in any part of this policy shall bear the same meaning wherever it may appear.' The insurer has just not worked hard enough on simplifying the language to just say: the definitions in the policy contract also apply to the policy certificate.

Another health cover I have, from a different insurer, warns:

If a claim is in any way found to be fraudulent, or if any false statement, or declaration is made or used in support of such a claim, or if any fraudulent means or devices are used by the Insured Person or anyone acting on behalf of the Insured Person or any false or incorrect Disclosure to Information Norms to obtain any benefit under this Policy, then We may reserve the right to re-underwrite or cancel the Policy and all claims being processed shall be forfeited for all Insured Persons and all sums paid under this Policy shall be repaid to Us by You who shall be jointly liable for such repayment.

This is intimidating because it feels as if the insurer's entire legal department will hunt me down were I to twist the facts. But I would be equally frightened if the insurer had just said: We can cancel your insurance and seek compensation if you lie.

We all sometimes generate content in a mechanical fashion. I too am guilty of this, as are our content writers churning out material on insurance to improve our website's chances of showing up on online searches. An insurer sent a letter to a friend cancelling her health insurance for non-disclosure of required information. Sections of the Insurance Act that she had violated were quoted, but then she was cheerfully assured of the insurer's absolute best services and a healthy life. In October each year, before my grandfather's birthday, insurers call my mother to wish and recommend that my grandfather buy term insurance immediately to avoid a price increase after his birthday. Were he to be alive today, my grandfather would be 108 years old, so my mother just tells the telemarketers that he is not taking calls anymore.

Technology can be a problem. Renewal notices come thick and fast before the renewal date with the disclaimer 'ignore this letter if you have already paid your premium'. This is a source of concern for many that have already paid their renewal premiums. The worry is that the insurer may not have registered the renewal payment and the policy could lapse. But the issue most often is that the insurer is unable to reconcile payments fast enough to stop future notices from going out.

Too much information obfuscates. In traditional life insurance, two important considerations are the expected returns on maturity and surrender. This information needs to be calculated from the extensive data in illustrations and is not highlighted. Similarly, in a home insurance the meaning of phrases such as 'market value' are not explained. The phrase implies that the free-market cost is insured. But actually it is the book value after adjusting for depreciation and can be much less than the cost of repair or replacement.

Your best solution to this mindlessness is, well, mindfulness. Mindfulness can be learnt. A few years ago, I would not have noticed single-use plastic in a poster. It took just one gritty Swedish teenager crisscrossing the Atlantic in a boat to make me more mindful.

You must read the contract you get, particularly the sections on benefits, exclusions and warranties. Think about situations that you might face in the future and how insurers may react, based on the contract wordings. When in doubt, write to the insurer asking for clarification. This extra effort when you buy the insurance will protect you from future claim rejection. However, sometimes there is just too much information in a policy contract for you to assimilate. Then what should you focus on?

The Devil Is in the Details

The thing about insurance is that you realize its value (or lack thereof) only when making a claim. A claim denied or not fully paid for a reason that you were unaware of, rankles. I get such complaints every day. People with the most severe grievances somehow tend to gravitate towards me to elaborately explain their problems! So, for your benefit, here are some conditions, footnotes and caveats that you should look for in your policy contract. You can prevent considerable heartburn and address these issues by asking the right questions while buying insurance rather than discovering the issues when making a claim.

- **Burglary insurance does not necessarily cover theft:** In insurance parlance burglary and theft are different. Burglary requires your house to be broken into, with the intention to steal. On the other hand, theft does not require forceful breaking in. A visitor to your home who pockets a piece of jewellery has committed theft and not burglary.

  Burglary insurance will cover theft only if explicitly mentioned in the contract. Theft insurance is more expensive, but still worth purchasing because it makes your insurance practical.

- **Motor insurance covers stolen vehicles only if you have the original keys:** Insurers ask for original keys as proof that you were not negligent in maintaining the security of the vehicle. If, like me, you have lost your original keys and have had a makeshift pair made by the local locksmith, then you are in for trouble if your vehicle gets stolen.

- **Fire insurance's sum assured reduces each year unless explicitly stated otherwise:** Consider a case where you purchase fire insurance for your home for ₹1 crore and renew it each year. On the fifth year your house burns down. You would expect to be paid ₹1 crore. Correct? Wrong. If your policy does not explicitly mention that value is estimated on reinstatement basis then you will be paid the original sum assured less depreciation, even though the cost of reconstruction may have increased substantially. This issue can be easily addressed by having a reinstatement value clause inserted in your contract.

- **Professional Indemnity insurance's effective cover could be a fraction of what you think it is:** Doctors, lawyers and chartered accountants are the most frequent purchasers of professional indemnity insurance. They pick their sum assured based on the exposure they face in their professions. However, most professionals are unaware that their insurance has an Any one Accident (AoA): Any one Year (AoY) ratio. This ratio determines the maximum amount that an insurer will pay in the case of any one accident. For example, if the ratio is 1:2 then the maximum liability that the insurer will pay in any one case is half the sum assured. It is common to have 1:2 or 1:3 as the specified ratio. As a result, quite often, the professional has much less insurance than they think they have.

Limits of this kind have been at the heart of insurance-related litigation related to the 9/11 event in the US. Insurers argued that the fall of the two World Trade Towers was one single event and so should be subject to the Any one Accident limit of USD 3.5 billion. The insured argued that these were two discrete events, with both towers being hit separately (and collapsing), hence the entire claim of USD 7.0 billion was payable. The final rulings in this litigation are complex. For some insurers the courts have treated the loss as one event but for others, as two. The difference is because of the way the questions were framed in the different proposal forms. I would advise you to keep your insurance simple and ask for a per-accident sublimit that is equal to the total sum assured, which means an AoA:AoY ratio of 1:1.

This is not an exhaustive list of conditions to be aware of. But there are three things to do when you buy insurance: ask questions before you write the cheque, read the policy mindfully, and do not hesitate to push back the insurer who denies your claim.

PART 4

Purpose

9

Why Insurance Exists

We Face Tremendous Risks

As a child I loved a Nintendo video game called *Oil Panic*. In this, a hapless young man hurtles from one side of the screen to another averting crisis after crisis. Come to think of it, this continues to be a common theme across games even today—fearlessly averting surprises and crises. Real life is no different.

We face risks every single day. Many of the adverse consequences of these risks can be insured away. To illustrate, I'll describe the risks I face in Delhi where I live (but other large cities are no different).

- 15,000+ COVID-19 cases per day. This was during the pandemic. Fortunately, as I despatch this book these numbers have subsided. A considerable proportion of people were treated at home but, for those admitted, the bills were steep. When my son was hospitalized for COVID-19 the expenses were over ₹2 lakh.

- **1,500** or more persons are diagnosed with acute respiratory, diarrhoeal diseases and tuberculosis every day. Some of these diseases require hospitalization but others, like tuberculosis, may require extended home treatment. A close family member's asthma gets aggravated each year as the air quality dips. A staff member had to leave us and return to her village because of tuberculosis. According to the National Health Profile, there are many other ailments that Delhiites are diagnosed with every day, I have just picked a few.

- **460** thefts and burglaries each day. These are the officially reported cases and I suppose the number of unreported cases is fairly large. Many of these burglaries involve loss of valuables; cash and jewellery being most common. My wife has an eye centre and a few years ago burglars stole all the air conditioners and other appliances worth about ₹1.5 lakh. Fortunately, the more expensive medical equipment was left untouched.

- **126** vehicles are stolen each day on Delhi roads. These can cost several lakhs. Some of these cars are forced open and taken away but there are a large number of cases where the vehicles are left unlocked, often with the keys in the motor vehicle!

- **85** fire calls are made every day to the fire department and the city has five fire-related injuries or deaths daily. A number of minor fires go unreported. People suffer burns in these fires and their homes get damaged. Sometimes, such as in the fire at the Natural History Museum, entire buildings get razed. A few months ago, during a heavy downpour, we had a minor fire in the electricity board at our home. This cost us ₹1 lakh to repair, even though the external work was done for free by the electricity company, BSES.

- **54** cancer cases are diagnosed each day in Delhi. This is dated information from the National Cancer Registry but the numbers have not reduced in recent years. Cancer shakes families up. My close relatives have paid up to ₹20 lakh for treatment of breast cancer.
- **15** road accidents took place in Delhi every day in 2019. This would have reduced materially during the lockdown but the number is still high.
- **14** heinous crimes are reported daily as per the Delhi Police 2019 records. Heinous crimes include rape, murder and attempts to murder. These crimes almost always result in injury, if not death.
- **3** earthquakes every 2 days, measuring over 5 on the Richter scale, are felt across the country. Quite a few of these are in the north according to the National Centre for Seismology. Earthquakes damage property and, in some poorly constructed homes, complete collapse may take place.

These estimates are taken from various sources, across years and are indicative. You could, like that hapless young man in *Oil Panic*, be anxiously alert for the next crisis to hit. Or you could act and buy the most essential insurances that give peace of mind, at least for monetary losses.

The four insurances that you must have are term, health, motor and home. Term will pay your nominee a large amount if you die. For a forty-year-old, a sum assured of ₹1 crore would cost ₹25,000 annually. Health insurance will pay your hospitalization costs. For the same forty-year-old to cover a family of four with ₹10 lakh will also cost about ₹25,000 per year. Motor insurance for a mid-sized car will be about ₹7,000 per year. This will pay for road accidents or stolen cars. Finally, home insurance for a mid-sized home will be ₹8,000 per year and will cover earthquake and fire-related costs. The total insurance cost is about ₹65,000 per year—a small investment to manage your risks.

Insurance Eliminates Many of Our Risks

A few years ago I received a New Year's WhatsApp greeting from Kalu. He was a poor worker who had been insured through a Trust that bought health insurance from us. I remember Kalu's case well. For the first four months of that group insurance, there were no claims, despite the number of insured members being large. On investigation, we found that workers lacked the confidence to walk into private hospitals, and when they did muster up the courage, they were turned away from the reception. To set this right I requested my father to accompany Kalu, then suffering from kidney disease, to the hospital and help him get past the formalities. Subsequently, Kalu's surgery was successfully completed, a kidney removed and the hospital bill of ₹85,000 paid for by insurance. Four years later, Kalu obviously felt cheerful enough to send me a video of flowers blooming in time-lapse.

I narrate this incident because it illustrates the purpose of insurance, which is to pay claims. The number of claims paid is significant. In the fiscal year 2020 to 2021 there were about 5,900 death claims; 38,000 health claims; and 72,000 general insurance claims paid every single day. Behind these statistics are stories that are often not told or understood, even by many within the industry itself. This is a major reason why job attrition in the insurance sector is so high. There are over 200,000 people working in insurance and at least 60,000 of them change jobs each year. In the sales teams that interact with customers, attrition rates are far higher. Such high attrition takes its toll. Policy lapses and complaints shoot up when the person that made the sale leaves. A stable employee-base leads to higher insurance renewal and pushes the company to keep improving its products. The best insurers in the world have staff that routinely spend the majority of their life working at the same company.

In exit interviews executives often point to the stigma associated with insurance. They complain about facing brickbats from unhappy clients, and family pressure to get into other professions. There seems to be a complete lack of understanding of the larger view, the main purpose of why they sell insurance. These executives may just as well have been selling any other financial product. When people understand the true value of insurance they stay for long, push the company to develop more customer-friendly products and have a positive impact on clients. Appreciating the true value of insurance can galvanize action.

As mentioned earlier, I once asked an extremely successful insurance salesperson in New Jersey what the turning point in his career was. He said that twenty years ago at a social gathering, a relative turned away when he approached. That is when he decided that he would work so hard to sell good insurance packages to his customers that one day the relative would approach him, unsolicited, for advice. This did eventually happen.

Good claims advice has real impact. Four years ago, a batchmate from business school called. She had ovarian cancer but her health insurer declined the claim because she had not disclosed her medical history properly when buying the insurance. We discussed this and drafted a response to her insurer where she apologized for the non-disclosure but also pointed out that the current ailment was medically unrelated to her non-disclosure. To the insurer's credit, they decided to settle the claim.

There are many such stories. I remember a decisive moment ten years ago when a salesperson sold life insurance to a subedar in the army. The subedar wrote out the cheque but tragically died in an accidental explosion before underwriting could be initiated. In that case the insurer made an ex gratia payment even though there was no claim payable. There are hundreds of such admirable stories that get buried in corporate busyness.

If the people who join insurance would only realize the impact they can have if they persevere and put their client's interest first, I doubt they would ever leave the industry. This was reinforced when the colleague I described earlier, called again. It turned out that her cancer treatments had failed, she had just a few months to live, but wanted to thank me properly for the help on her claim several years ago. In that moment, she made my work special and reminded me of the purpose of insurance.[54]

How Insurance Gives Dignity

Her body lay unclaimed for forty-eight hours. Her children had brought her to the hospital. After five days of intensive medical care, she died, and her family could not afford the ₹50,000 hospital bill. Somebody did finally step in to pay and she was properly cremated.

This incident took place six years ago but came back vividly to my mind when I heard a well-known academician identify lack of personal dignity as one of India's biggest issues.

Indignity is all around us. It is there when your domestic staff goes broke because someone falls ill in their family, when someone yells at the waiter in a restaurant or when we must wait interminably for VIP chief guests to arrive. People with mental illnesses are looked down upon, executives out of a job face this, and the disabled suffer when they find themselves at the doorsteps of buildings they cannot climb.

Why do I mention dignity in a book on insurance? Because the core issue here is the lack of financial independence and insurance can address this. Take the disturbing example I just cited. This is a common enough issue in South Africa where the quality of burial is an important measure of a life's worth. Insurers there address this by selling funeral plans. These are low-value term plans issued without medical tests, that pay just enough to cover the last rites or any terminal medical expenses. The death benefit is paid within hours of the person dying. Several insurers also take care of funeral arrangements. The poor in India have similar needs for terminal emergency care and last rites. That hospital bill of ₹50,000 could well have been paid by a term plan costing less than ₹200 per year .

Many years ago, I would often visit my aunt who lived in South Delhi. On the ground floor of her building, outside the house, there was always an old, infirm man on a charpoy, cheerfully reading an Urdu newspaper. I learnt that his family had thrown the old man out to take care of himself. Look carefully and such examples will jump out at you frequently.

In the US and Europe, long-term care and assisted-living insurances are sold. These insurances step in if you are bedridden or need daily care. In India, most elderly have no option but to depend upon their family for daily care. That bedridden, newspaper-reading neighbour would have had a lot more dignity were he not dependent on his family and could afford a proper home and a caregiver.

The rich suffer indignity too. An increasingly common, though not fully appreciated, predicament is of senior executives losing their jobs. This shakes them up and turns their financial planning upside down because they thought they would retire at sixty-five not forty-five. This is effectively twenty years of living on a reduced income, because most never again get comparable high-paying jobs. To compound the social stigma, many executives have managed their finances and insurances poorly. Such executives want to port their company health and life insurances to themselves. Unfortunately, these options are limited.

People with mental illness also face difficulties. Some estimates suggest that about 10 per cent of the population suffers from some form of mental illness. India has just about 9,000 psychiatrists, which is a quarter of the requirement[55]. This makes psychiatric treatment expensive. There are a larger number of psychologists and counsellors but these are also well below required levels. Also, most insurers will not issue you insurance even if you have mild mental ill-health. Insurers should expand cover to pay for mental health OPD. They should create a panel of psychiatrists that are acceptable or define clear standards for mental illness, the way they have for many critical illnesses. This will encourage people to visit credible doctors and not hide the issue.

Finally, life insurance should take on a more meaningful role in creating small savings. However, this will require a meaningful change in product structures. First, returns need to be far higher than the 2 to 6 per cent offered today on traditional insurances. Second, cash withdrawals must be easier and less expensive.

Years ago, while in school, I learnt how small savings lead to dignity. When I needed money, I just had to show a report card to my grandmother. She could not read very well but understood that a reward was called for. Carefully, with a toothy smile, she would unroll a wad of notes hidden deep in the layers of her Rubia cotton suits and give me fifty rupees. She smiled because she could afford to give me money without asking anyone. I must confess that, sometimes, I may have shown her the same examination marks twice to get more rewards. Had she known, she would have happily forgiven me. That is what financial independence can do.[56]

Notes

1   The IBAI survey was of a small group but it's reflective of how you should think about health insurance. A Net Promoter Score (NPS) approach (described in the endnote 2) was used. The brokers surveyed had deep knowledge of health insurance, and over 66 per cent of them had more than half their clients buying health insurance. The main observations were: (a) that product features were the most important factor in making a health insurance purchase (NPS score 53 per cent), followed by price (24 per cent) and claims settlement (24 per cent). (b) Product features like low pre-existing exclusion period (NPS score 82 per cent) and no room-rent capping (NPS score 66 per cent) were most important. Features such as high no-claim bonus (NPS score 16 per cent), critical-illness cover (NPS score 13 per cent) were moderately important. However, wellness benefits (NPS score of -29 per cent) and international cover (NPS score of -34 per cent) were not deciding factors in the purchase decision. The reason for poor ratings in wellness and international cover was that claims in these areas were few. (c) In all, 32 per cent of the brokers surveyed were highly satisfied with the health insurance

claims settlement rate, whereas 29 per cent are not satisfied. The remaining are moderately satisfied. (d) Brokers feel there is room for improvement when it comes to health insurance grievance handling, only 4 per cent of the brokers surveyed were satisfied with it, whereas 35 per cent brokers rated it 'not satisfied'. (e) Only 24 per cent of the brokers surveyed were highly satisfied with the medical test and policy issuance process, whereas 42 per cent were 'not satisfied'.

2   In the Net Promoter Score (NPS) survey, a 10-point scale is used. Promoters are those that give a score of 9 or 10, detractors those that gave 6 or less. The NPS is the difference between promoters and detractors. Read more about the NPS in Fred Reichheld & Rob Markey, *The Ultimate Question 2.0: How Net Promoter Companies Thrive in a Customer-Driven World* (Boston, MA: Harvard Business Press, 2011).

3   I am referring to the health insurance ratings done by us in collaboration with *moneycontrol* in 2022. Prior to this we worked on the health insurance ratings with the *Mint* newspaper between 2013 and 2020. In our health insurance ratings, every single individual health insurance is scored on a fact-based scale that covers pricing, product features and claims. Products are classified as A, B or C. The MCSHIR provides a rational approach to discussing and understanding health insurance products. You will find some references to the MCSHIR throughout this book. The detailed methodology and results can be read on: https://securenow.in/specials/mediclaim-ratings-insurance. Deepti Bhaskaran, mentioned also in the Acknowledgements, has been a steady collaborator in all the health insurance ratings that SecureNow has done.

4   I learnt about algorithms, operations research and much more from Prof. Kiran Seth, Padma Shree Awardee & Professor Emeritus at IIT Delhi. Little did he realize the impact his Wednesday afternoon classes, in an isolated corner of the IIT building, had on us young students.

5   The complete ratings and the methodology can be seen on: https://securenow.in/specials/mediclaim-ratings-insurance.

6   The detailed ratings can be read on: https://securenow.in/specials/mediclaim-ratings-insurance.

7   *IRDAI Annual Report*, FY2021

8   With medical advancements, diseases such as Alzheimer's can be detected well before onset through blood tests. This creates an ethical dilemma. If insurance applicants are high risk will they be denied an insurance cover? Or will they be charged an additional premium? Such ethical issues are also inherent in DNA testing that is rapidly gaining ground. Read https://www.nytimes.com/2020/07/28/health/alzheimers-blood-test.html to learn about the progress in identifying Alzheimer's.

9   This exclusion is illogical. A person diagnosed with a severe condition that results in immediate death will not be paid, but someone with a less severe critical illness will be. Ideally, this requirement for survival after developing a critical illness should be done away with.

10   This section was originally written in February 2019 well before the pandemic. Now the statistics will be even more skewed because incidence of other illnesses such as heart attacks or strokes appears to have fallen, while COVID-related illnesses have increased substantially.

11   The IRDAI issued guidelines Ref. No.: IRDAI/HLT/REG/CIR/177/09/2019 on Standardization of Exclusions in Health Insurance Contracts in September 2019. These guidelines are extremely policyholder-friendly and do not allow for many exclusions. For example, oral chemotherapy that was often excluded as a treatment for cancer can no longer be left out.

12   'Higher quality, Lower Costs: India's Cancer Grid Promise' available at https://the-ken.com/story/higher-quality-lower-costs-indias-cancer-grid-promise on 4 July 2019.

13   'Breast Cancer Landscape in India', published by the Confederation of Indian Industry (CII), in association with the Indian Council of Medical Research (ICMR), National Institute of Cancer Prevention And Research (NICPR) and Novartis International AG, a Swiss multinational pharmaceutical company—in October 2018.

14   This was McKinsey & Company, which like Hindustan Lever where I also worked, really invests in developing people. Both companies have generated a long line-up of CEOs. I may still not be able to leap over tall buildings in one go but am willing to give it a shot.

15   I had moments of anxiety several years ago when my term insurance application was turned down by an insurer. At that

time medical reports were not shared with applicants but, because the insurer knew me, they did send me the reports. There was nothing alarming in the health report but the jolt forced me to shed a few kilo and when I applied a few months later the insurance was issued. Today, the standard process is to share a copy of the medical reports with the buyers so they can see why an insurance is rejected or "loaded," meaning the premium is increased.

16	There are over 65 million diabetics and over 7 per cent of adults suffer from this disease. See India State-Level Disease Burden Initiative Diabetes Collaborators, 'The Increasing Burden of Diabetes and Variations Among the States of India: the Global Burden of Disease Study 1990–2016', *The Lancet Global Health* 6, no. 12 (December 2018): E1352–E1362, available at doi: 10.1016/S2214-109X(18)30387-5. Diabetes is a huge, not fully recognized issue.

17	At the time of writing, Star Health was the only insurer covering Type 1 diabetes, including for senior citizens through various specialized products.

18	Cancer cover is offered by HDFC Life, Max Life and ICICI Prudential amongst others. Dengue cover is available from HDFC Ergo Health.

19	Section 45, Insurance Act 1938, (Incorporating all amendments including the amendment by the Finance (No.2) Act, 2019). Section 45 states that: 'Policy will not be called in question on ground of misstatement after three years. —(1) No policy of life insurance shall be called in question on any ground whatsoever after the expiry of three years from the date of the policy, i.e., from the date of issuance of the policy or the date of commencement of risk or the date of revival of the policy or the date of the rider to the policy, whichever is later'.

20	IRDAI/HLT/REG/CIR/152/06/2020.		Guidelines		on Standardization of General Terms and Clauses in Health Insurance Policy Contracts. Section 12 on the Moratorium Period states:

> After completion of eight continuous years under the policy no look back to be applied. This period of eight years is called as moratorium period. The moratorium would be applicable for the sums insured of the first policy and subsequently on completion of 8 continuous

years would be applicable from date of enhancement of sums insured only on the enhanced limits. After the expiry of Moratorium Period no health insurance claim shall be contestable except for proven fraud and permanent exclusions specified in the policy contract. The policies would however be subject to all limits, sub limits, co-payments, deductibles as per the policy contract.

21 IRDAI/HLT/REG/ClR/046/02/2020, Amendments in respect of provisions of Guidelines on Standardization of Exclusions in Health Insurance Contracts and Modification Guidelines on Standardization in Health Insurance. The definition of pre-existing conditions used to be open-ended, allowing a disease to be classified as pre-existing even if signs and symptoms existed before the insurance was bought, but the condition had not been diagnosed. In an important revision, this definition was changed by the IRDAI and standardized across products. The standard definition is:

> Pre-existing Disease means any condition, ailment, injury or disease: a) That is/are diagnosed by a physician within 48 months prior to the effective date of the policy issued by the insurer or its reinstatement or b) For which medical advice or treatment was recommended by, or received from, a physician within 48 months Prior to the effective date of the policy issued by the insurer or its reinstatement.

This was a step forward because it clarified that a disease diagnosis should have been made, or a doctor should have recommended treatment within the four years preceding an insurance purchase for the disease to be considered pre-existing. It was not sufficient for just the symptoms of the disease to exist.

22 The David and Goliath allegory is apt. We feel intimated about taking on large insurers but if you are in the right, like David, you will eventually win. Insurers will often settle when you reach out to the ombudsman or take legal action.

23 Insurers and hospitals just do not see eye-to-eye. Insurers are of the view that hospitals materially overcharge and hospitals find insurers overbearing in areas they (the insurers) do not understand. My experience is in insurance but my wife and several close friends are doctors. I appreciate both perspectives

which is why in writing this chapter, I also highlight the issues that the medical fraternity face.

24   There is an opportunity here for a company that can cut this discharge time from hours to minutes. Much of the communication between the insurer, TPA, hospital, doctor and patient is over email. This can be done real-time but an independent party, not linked to hospitals or insurers, will need to take the lead. There are two projects currently underway on this. The first by the Insurance Information Bureau (IIB) and the second by the National Health Mission. These projects are difficult to execute but can dramatically improve the patient's experience of discharge.

25   Refer to IRDAI's circular dated 11 June 2020: 'Modified Guidelines on Product filing in Health Insurance Business-Norms on Proportionate Deductions', available at https://www.irdai.gov.in/ADMINCMS/cms/whatsNew_Layout.aspx?page=PageNo4156&flag=1.

26   This was Hindustan Lever, now Hindustan Unilever. I was in my first job as an Area Sales Manager responsible for Telangana, stretching from Hyderabad to Adilabad. On trips into the country the bosses would settle down into the Ambassador car and begin asking questions the moment we left the city. Many of these questions were about what they saw outside and their way of determining whether I had worked the 'market'. When I look back, I shudder at the answers I gave, and I am thankful for their kindness at not bursting into laughter at them. It was and is a fabulous company.

27   The IRDAI issued a circular Ref. No: IRDA/HLT/MISC/CIR/128/08/2018 in response to the Mental Healthcare Act, 2017. The Act required that as per Sec 21(4), 'every insurer shall make provision for medical insurance for treatment of mental illness on the same basis as is available for treatment of physical illness.' This circular does not mean that persons with mental illness must be provided health insurance but that, if the insurer does give insurance, then hospitalization costs related to mental ill-health have to be covered. Practically, insurers will seldom issue insurance to people with metal illness.

28   The insurance regulator in July 2020 nudged insurers to launch a standard Corona Rakshak insurance that pays a fixed benefit if you are tested Covid-19 positive. Pricing has been left to

insurers. The same notification had also mandated that insurers launch a Corona Kavach insurance, which is indemnity-based for Covid-19. This insurance covers Personal Protection Equipment (PPE), diagnostic costs and home quarantine costs as well. In that sense these are more comprehensive for Covid-19 than standard mediclaim insurances. However, their limitation is that these are not renewable lifelong and the insurance is restricted to just COVID-19 and related complications. These insurances are now in the market, but there are wide price variations between insurers. You must compare prices before buying, because the benefits are identical across insurers but the prices are not.

29   Some of the insurers that cover cancer, cardiac issues and diabetes are Star Health, Care Health and HDFC Ergo. Adventure sports are covered by Bajaj General and emergency care for pre-existing conditions while travelling overseas is covered by Care insurance. There are others as well that would cover these risks so this list is illustrative.

30   A special mention to the Caddies Welfare Trust (CWT) that organized this insurance and, for five years, has successfully run this programme free for caddies who are all daily wage earners.

31   A circular specifying the format and rules for illustration was published by the IRDAI on 26 September 2019. Ref: IRDAI/ LIFE/Circ/Misc/173/09/2019

32   The Aadhaar card has been a blessing because it allows the basic KYC to be done in a seamless manner. For several years the Supreme Court had prohibited insurers and other institutions from using Aadhaar. However, that restriction has now been removed and this considerably simplifies the purchase process. The IRDAI, through a circular—Ref. No: IRDAI/Life/Cir/ Misc/208/08/2020—allowed life insurers to do away with a physical signature on proposal forms and use alternate ways of verification such as an OTP or link-based acceptance. This waiver is due to the COVID-19 situation that makes physical signatures difficult, and is given until 31 December 2020. However, I do expect that this will be extended, because it is a practical substitute for physical signature verification.

33   In fact the IRDAI has gone a step further and prohibited life insurance claims from being rejected for any reason after three years have been completed (Section 45 of the 2019 Amended Insurance Act, 1938). This addresses some of the concerns

around simplified issue insurance. However, early deaths in the first three years are still subject to investigation and such claims are rejected if fraud is proven. There is ambiguity around what is fraud. The regulator has been steadily pushing for a high bar on declaring a life insurance purchase as fraud. This has worked to the benefit of policyholders but insurers are concerned about an increase in early claims that are fraudulent but difficult to prove. Previously this risk could be mitigated by longer-term death liens.

34   The ombudsman rulings over the years can be read on https://www.cioins.co.in/Awards. These are instructive and useful to understand the issues that come about in claims and other benefits.

35   I am referring to SelectQuote founder, Charan Singh. SelectQuote operates in the US and sells only pure risk insurances. For many years this was just term insurance and more recently health insurance was added. In May 2020, in the midst of the pandemic lockdown, SelectQuote completed an IPO that valued the company at over USD 3 billion. This shows that large businesses can be built around protection-oriented insurance. I did eventually manage to get Charan into India indirectly, through an investment in SecureNow.

36   Section 13 on Minimum Guaranteed Interest Rate in Insurance Regulatory and Development Authority of India (Unit-Linked Insurance Products) Regulations, 2019. Dated 8 July 2019.

37   Section 20 on Surrender Charge in Insurance Regulatory and Development Authority of India (Non-Linked Insurance Products) Regulations, 2019. Dated 8 July 2019.

38   Chapter 9 on Surrender Value in the Insurance Regulatory and Development Authority of India (Non-Linked Insurance Products) Regulations, 2019. Dated 8 July 2019.

39   Section 21 in Insurance Regulatory and Development Authority of India (Non-Linked Insurance Products) Regulations, 2019 dated 8 July 2019 and Insurance Regulatory and Development Authority of India (Unit Linked Insurance Products) Regulations, 2019 dated 8 July 2019. A higher annuitization of accumulated funds is allowed. However, given the relatively low annuity returns and taxes on annuities, most prefer to commute or take out their funds tax-free as much as possible without buying an annuity.

40   Over the past few years critical-illness insurances have evolved
      to cover diseases such as Alzheimer's and strokes both of which
      may not require extensive hospitalization. These then are good
      complements to a standard medical insurance.

41   *Annual Report 2019–20*, Insurance Regulatory and Development
      Authority of India

42   Insurance Ombudsman Rules, 2017 published by the Department
      of Financial Services, Insurance Division, New Delhi, 25 April
      2017. The rules specify that individuals, micro-enterprises
      and sole proprietors can complain to the ombudsmen but not
      other companies. The decision of the ombudsman is binding on
      insurers, but not on individuals who can thereafter reach out to
      other courts if they do not accept the award.

43   In mid-2019, a fire broke out at a coaching centre in Surat killing
      many children. The loss of life was tragic, compounded by the
      fact that the authorities did not see the obvious. Reducing fire
      hazards is the first priority, getting insurance the second.

44   The complete claims handbook can be downloaded from
      https://securenow.in/blog/general-insurance-claims-insights-a-
      policyholders-handbook/

45   The complete results for 2020 can be read on https://securenow.
      in/blog/ibai-broker-friendly-insurers-survey/. The 2021 and
      2022 results that are being referred to here can be acquired by
      emailing support@securenow.in.

46   IRDAI's FY2021 annual report

47   I can't help but laugh when I think of this fierce commando at the
      MG Road metro station in Gurugram. The irony is that, despite
      the stern warning, dozens of commuters would still walk up,
      glare into the muzzle of the machine gun and ask for directions
      to Rajiv Chowk metro station.

48   Our sales persons find it very difficult to say no to clients. Buyers
      can be irrational and expect sales persons to twist the rules for
      them. The phrase used is to make an 'exception'. In insurance
      such exceptions generally do not end well.

49   This was a home in the hills that was being insured. We went
      through 'Babbles', 'Blooble' and 'Bangle' before getting the
      name right. Each change requiring an unnecessary week or two.

50   This was Tony Singh, the CEO at Max New York Life, where
      I worked in insurance for the first time. He is one of the three

people to whom this book is dedicated. The other two being Charan Singh of SelectQuote and Bob Fallon of Prudential.

51   Section 39, Insurance Act 1938, (Incorporating all amendments including the amendment by the Finance (No.2) Act, 2019).

52   Tayal versus United India case, February 2018, Delhi High Court, Justice Pratibha Singh.

53   Guidelines on Standardization of Exclusions in Health Insurance Contracts, 27 September 2019.

54   Kalu continues to be a caddie at the Delhi Golf Club covered under a group health insurance organized by the Caddies Welfare Trust. He is active on the course, ferrying golfers around. The friend described in the last paragraph died from cancer. At our IIM Ahmedabad twenty-fifth reunion, she was fondly remembered and missed.

55   K. Garg, C.N. Kumar and P.S. Chandra, 'Number of Psychiatrists in India: Baby Steps Forward, but a Long Way to Go', *Indian Journal of Psychiatry* 61, no. 1 (2019): 104–05, available at 10.4103/psychiatry.IndianJPsychiatry_7_18.

56   I did not attach much significance to the rewards that my grandmother gave me. It's only now so many years after she has died that I think about the significance of small sums of money saved up for a rainy day or to help others. These are some things one appreciates with age.

Index

Acknowledgements

To Tony Singh, who pulled me out from consulting into insurance. A long time ago, in 2003, he brushed aside dissent to hire me into Max New York Life, a decision that I remain forever grateful for. From Tony I learnt how to listen to all but ultimately take one's own decision.

To Bob Fallon, my friend and one-time boss. As I built a life insurance business for Prudential in India, Bob always had my back. Come what may I could count on him, and still do to this day.

To Charan Singh, the most inspiring entrepreneur I know, and his lovely wife Sylvia, co-creators of SelectQuote, the fabulous US-based insurance distribution business they built. A major reason for my decision to become an entrepreneur was to emulate Charan. I'm incredibly proud that Charan is also an investor in SecureNow.

To Monika Halan, for creating a platform within *Mint* where I wrote on insurance for over a decade. That's the first time I realized that readers loved personal stories so much more than cold facts! A special thanks to Monika, herself a successful author on personal finance, for introducing me to her wonderful editor at HarperCollins.

To Sachin Sharma, the wonderful editor that I refer to above. He is blunt and I'm grateful for that. Years of business writing has made my style antiseptic. Sachin thoughtfully explained why books are different from boardroom presentations. The credit for fine-tuning the title and theme go to him. As also for making the structure and overall communication more engaging for readers. Without Sachin's active help, the book would have read like a research report. That's not a bad thing in itself, but a rather ineffective way to reach out to general readers.

To Sashi Aiyer and Pooja Sanyal, for painstakingly reading and improving the manuscript, including the very detailed footnotes. Full credit to Sashi and Pooja for going deep into the subject and helping me communicate, the way I wanted to, in the book. Thank you, Gavin Morris, for designing a beautiful cover that evocatively captures the essence of insurance.

To the Insurance Brokers Association of India, where I have been an elected director for several years now. The passion with which all the directors have taken up policyholder issues is wonderful. I've discussed many of the examples in this book with my director colleagues and without exception their view has always been that policyholders come first.

To Deepti Bhaskaran, seasoned journalist, with whom I have worked extensively on insurance matters. In 2011, when she was at *Mint*, I gave my first write-up to her. Within hours she got back, telling me that I had written an article when she wanted a column. From her feedback over the years I learnt to tell personal stories on insurance and not always be bound by mundane data tables to explain a point. If you remained awake while reading this book the credit goes to Deepti.

To Abhishek, who co-founded SecureNow with me, in 2011. I started my entrepreneurial journey after having been a chief executive for some years. I thought that building SecureNow would be easy, but this has by far been one of the hardest things for me. There is no way we would have reached the stage we are at now, if I had not teamed up with Abhishek. Every minute of building SecureNow has been a joy, for which much of the credit goes to him.

To Veena, my mother, for never once in all my life letting me feel that I was not exceptional. Through ups and downs, thick and thin, she has unflinchingly backed me, including by investing money when much was at risk.

To Ravi, my father, for being my most sincere follower. He has clipped every article I've ever written and that's quite a few, systematically filing them in a physical 'Kapil' folder. When we started SecureNow and needed an additional licensed person for regulatory reasons, he studied for the mandatory hundred hours and took the brokers' license exam, which he passed with flying colours—all this for me, when he was seventy-four.

To Salt and Chip, my four-legged friends. Salt was with me in the beginning and Chip in the end.

To Tamanna and Aditya, my wonderful children. Tamanna has this extraordinary knack of forcing me to be less serious. She is the only person in the world who, when I am worried about something, will sit silently next to me and pull my cheeks to make me smile. She will also remind me that it's okay if what I write is not perfect. Her ability to read my mind is a sure sign that she will be an outstanding lawyer one day. Aditya has been my most meticulous editor. I would leave some writings on his study table and a few hours later get back detailed, specific and actionable comments. Very blunt but absolutely spot-on. He is a boy of few words but with such a compassionate nature, I'm quite sure that he will become a much-loved doctor.

Like Anjali, my wife, best friend and partner. She often sat by my side doing her own work as I laboured through the various drafts after work. When she sensed I was slowing down, Anjali would magically play a medley of my favourite songs. In large part, my drive to write comes from watching her juggle a thousand different things, from a busy medical practice to charitable work, to fighting for women's rights to writing for the papers herself. Many of Anjali's experiences fill this book and I couldn't have done this without her. Thank you.

About the Author

Kapil Mehta is the co-founder of SecureNow, an award-winning insurance broking firm that uses technology-based distribution to sell commercial insurances to MSMEs in India.

Kapil writes regularly in the media, specifically on matters that impact policyholders. He is a director of the Insurance Brokers Association of India, a policyholder representative on the Policyholder Protection Board Subcommittee of a life insurer and on the SME advisory board of a leading general insurer. He is also active in several industry associations and is a charter member of TiE.

Kapil was formerly the managing director of Prudential Financial's life insurance company in India. Still earlier, he worked with Max New York Life, McKinsey & Company and Unilever.

Kapil studied at IIM Ahmedabad and IIT Delhi. He adores *Calvin and Hobbes*, and playing with Chip, his dog. He took to constructing crosswords during the pandemic, after his attempt to make the family play bridge failed. His first crossword was published in October 2021. Kapil's wife is an eye surgeon, his elder daughter is studying law, and his younger son wants to be a doctor.